Coffee Cups
&
Wine Glasses

*Hilarious Secrets to Heal a Broken
Heart & Get Your Life Back!*

*Includes Life Hacks & Journal Prompts for
Happiness, Motivation, & Brilliant Entertainment.*

Debbie Seagle

Coffee Cups & Wine Glasses © Copyright <<2022>> DOIT Publishing

For more information: https://www.lifebackdoit.com.

ISBN: 978-1-958685-00-6

DISCLAIMER:

This is a book of true fiction. That means the stories are true, but most names have been changed to protect the innocent and the guilty and to confuse those who think they know who they are. RC: a fictitious character. I never knew Dick Head. Obviously.

It is written from a woman's perspective, intended to amuse and provoke thought, reflection, and healing. Any advice given in this book is an offering from someone with healthy battle scars and is not professional in the sense that educated theories are presented in any way. Inspiring buffoonery and whimsy however are my profession. So, you can take all of the enclosed self-deprecating disclosures as professionally tested solutions to finding a better way to live, improve, and enjoy your life.

Any user of anything I suggest assumes the full risk of insult, injury, embarrassment, and legal consequences resulting from performing any activity in this book. I will only be held accountable for my own actions. You do whatever makes you happy. Hopefully, everything you do from now on will make you happy!

Get Your Free Gift!

For the best experience with this book, readers who download and use the Free DOiT Journal have more fun, learn more about themselves, and don't have to write on cocktail napkins!

Get Your Free Journal on my website: www.lifebackdoit.com

If you enjoy *Coffee Cups & Wine Glasses,* I'd like to hear from you and hope you will post a review on Amazon. Your review only counts after you've flipped through to the end of an eBook. Your feedback and support are important to me, especially if you were able to laugh while Getting Your Life Back!

Table of Contents

Preamble

Mother Teresa said that one of the ways to practice Humility is to accept being slighted, forgotten, and disliked.

I'm practicing. You probably are too. But we can change that, and become glorious with humility, while still being humble. Appreciate your magnificence and Get Your Life Back – DOiT.

Reading Instructions

By falling into this book, you will become skilled in dodging, slamming into, and laughing at the unwelcome changes life throws at you. Every chapter reveals recipes, outlandish skills, or activities to enrich your life with whimsey and flair, much like a life hack.

A "Life Hack" is a clever trick to provide simple solutions to life's frustrations … Like getting your Life Back.

A "DOIT" is an obsolete Dutch coin of little value. But when you DOiT, you will gain significant value.

Hence: the discoveries at the end of every chapter are your *"Life-Back-DOiTs."* You are encouraged to try them (for free). They are a valuable wealth of knowledge for your pleasure, confidence and absurdity. So, when you reach the end of every chapter, just DOiT. Get it?

Congratulations! You are among the first to implement

"Life-Back-DOiTs" to become a human genius!

(Wine glass raised here.)

Sample DOiT:

Take A Stuffed Animal to The Vet. Be all freaked out about his condition, and tell everyone how much he means to you. Call him by his name and talk to him to calm him down. Be sure to escape before they call someone to lock you up.

OK, that was a bad example, but you get the idea. DOiTs are usually useful, but sometimes silly.

DOiT Journal.

Writing helps you clear your head and own up to the fact that you are the one making decisions about what you think ... and want ... and do. DOiT while you're still sober. If it's too late for that, write it anyway! That may be more fun to look back on.

A prompt after every chapter encourages you to reach inside yourself to reveal your buried self-wisdom and intuitions to Get Your Life Back. DOiT darlin' (If you want to).

Footnotes:

THEY:

The experts who know everything, as in "THEY say"

RC:

I didn't want to Dick-up this book too much, so to clarify the references to RC on the following pages:

RC stands for Richard Cranium. (Dick-Head).

(Richard = Dick) (Cranium = Head) – my RC or yours, just a Dick Head.

Potato-Smasher-Word:

Write inspiring words on pieces of paper to hang from your potato-smasher with colorful twine or yarn. I'll point out a few as we go. Sounds crazy you say? Think of it as a hanging vision mobile. You're smashing; so, keep searching for something good and smash it! (In a good way.) Besides, it gives you something to do with your hands between drinking sessions.

Introduction

Where I'm coming from, and where you may not want to go…

"Confidence is needed to proceed, and Humility is the way to build confidence."
~*Debbie Craig*

Dogs sometimes eat shit. That's funny; I don't know why. But saying it is comical … "eat shit."

That doesn't mean I'm going to do it (anymore). I'm not a dog. I've had enough, and I proved it by dealing with the shambles of my marriage like a dog handles life: If you don't want to eat it or hump it, piss on it and walk away. So, I did.

But it's because of Richard Cranium (RC) that we're not sharing the life and family we built together. Now I only have myself to share 35 years of memories only RC and I found hilarious. We did share puberty, our first home in a ramshackle trailer on PFC pay, and a single 24 oz Fosters beer every payday to celebrate (payday). PFC is the Marine Corps rank: Private First Class and, back in the day, that was equivocal to $443 per month. If Private First Class sounds like a good wine, it will be soon! Details in the future on www.lifebackdoit.com.

At my first and only wedding, I promised "as long as we both shall live," and I really meant it. He was my true love. That's the reason I married him. That, and the fact that he could thaw a frozen pipe under a trailer home with a blow torch. He duct-taped our jeep tail light to pass inspection and could butcher a deer. That's how we survived our first few years of marriage. Those were the good ole days. I hardly recall how the good days turned bad, but they did, and I suddenly became the enemy.

Oh, I didn't recently get divorced. It has been years. It hit me after three years though, that I wasn't moving on. I thought I was evolving but was only emulating the roadrunner. Feet spinning, lots of dust, no progress ... then ... off the cliff. My life was a romantic comedy, without the romance.

I read somewhere that for each year of a relationship, you should expect one month of recovery after it ends. Part of that recovery process is about achieving distance and perspective ... Blah Blah Blah.

Honestly, that's true, but it sounded like dogshit the first time I heard it. I didn't care what anyone else thought I should do to forget the life I'd lost. No one could possibly understand.

That's why I've outlined a plan for you. (I recognize the irony here, but) I'm including useful skills in this book, Real Skills ... like how to fake your own death and where to hide the potato-smasher, and WHY. Plus, some things you probably shouldn't do. You may benefit from avoiding every situation in this book. For now, just get yourself a wonderful wine glass or coffee cup. It will temporarily fill the void and inspire your accomplishments throughout the remainder of this book.

Oh, grab your potato-smasher too.

Back in 1978, in Dublin, Virginia, population 5,576, when you walked into Contessa Beauty Shop, you were slapped in the face with an 11x17" portrait of Miss National Teen of Virginia in an enormous gilded frame. She is donning a banner and crown, leaning against a fence, gazing into the distance looking constipated.

It should have been easy to refrain from smiling (as the photographer insisted) at 7:30 the morning after accidentally winning the state title, but it wasn't. I only entered the pageant to make mom happy. She lived vicariously through me. I didn't even tell my friends about the contest because I didn't expect to win. It was RC's birthday, and I simply wanted to get home.

All I ever wanted from life existed in that one-stoplight town, just like all simple-minded kids in Dublin. We played kick the can until dark, climbed trees, and had secret hideouts. We got spankings from our dads (mine had a huge leather State Police belt), and we all had to be home for dinner and wash the dishes after we did our homework.

I don't know about the others, but I was smothered in unconditional love from my mom. Her perceptive attention was annoying then. But after she died of breast cancer, no one remembered my birthday for two years. No one called to warn me of mad cow disease, and no one told me how to do everything differently. I wasn't sure how to do anything anymore. Especially after a heartbreaking divorce.

So, after my divorce…

I went skydiving, horseback riding, fly fishing, and castrated a calf at a "Wild West Women" retreat in Montana. I *wined* a lot. Then I went on an all-woman hiking and ziplining week in Arizona; climbed to Angel's Landing, and lost 8 pounds eating vegan for six days. I flew with an airshow team to 42 airshows in two years, started an event planning (and of all things, wedding planning) business, and vowed to become more involved in the everyday life of my three grown sons. My boys weren't as enthused as I was about the idea. They had their own lives. So, I started mine.

I accepted a job in Japan a few months before the big tsunami; had brain surgery; got engaged and almost married a hunk of a man who adored me and wanted sex five times a day. I know, you're thinking, "shouldn't THAT be the story?" Hmmmm … maybe the next book. (Too Many Shades of Thank You.)

Before I knew about her, I spent six days alone in Paris after charges showed up on my credit card from RC's trip to Europe with his Texas Trash

Tramp on my birthday. I stayed in the hotel where they charged our credit card. (That strategy is not recommended.)

I identified as brave and adventurous. I still identified as a woman; but nonetheless, changed my persona from wife/mom to majestic unicorn. I deserved more than cold leftovers and a used mattress. I was single, free, and (learning to be) just me. I only had myself to answer to. The problem was, I didn't know the questions. Hopefully, you'll find your questions and answers in the following pages. If nothing else, you will learn to laugh and be entertained mindlessly.

When I got over the "I am woman, watch me soar" tour...

I unintentionally began to live my own life two steps forward, six stumbles back. THEY say setbacks are proof that you're making progress. Maybe THEY are full of it.

Here is what I did ... mindlessly ... coffee cup or wine glass in hand. (Usually a wine glass.)

If you're newly separated and want to focus on riding your own "I am woman, watch me soar" rollercoaster, skip to Chapter 18 and follow the 10 steps to Getting Over Dick Head.

Then come back to the beginning for more entertaining and ridiculous ideas to get your life back.

1

Escaping A Breakup with Your Potato-Smasher

"Humility, that low, sweet root, from which all heavenly virtues shoot."
~Thomas Moore

Who needs a bottle of wine when heartbreak can make you just as senseless? Even if you feel like you're eating soup with a fork, don't give up. Little dribbles of hope and clarity will seep into your journey as you follow along.

After being humiliated too many times, the conflict between what you know and what you feel can be resolved by looking at where you are. If it's where you want to be, then ... there you are. But if you're making a complete fool of yourself and torturing everyone in your life with your crazy pinball relationship woes, it's time to get out of the arcade and make your way to a new mecca.

First, give yourself some credit. You have become virtuous by continuing to breathe after your heart was crushed. Secondly, simply escape. If you're the type to stay and fight for what you want, you will discover when, or if, it's time to pack your bags, even if you don't know where to go.

Take charge of your itinerary. It's not easy, but you will find a way if you open your mind to all possible routes. I will help you.

I learned an ingenious tactic when I slid into an obscure hideout with a wave of relief. I had escaped. A new life began for me when I had my tolerance tested. It was negative. So were the emotions seeping from my marriage. It was time to go.

You probably don't know about the guarded secret I am about to expose. (I had a Top Secret clearance back then.) It was a passage to paradise, behind an obvious facade, veiled in plain view. I am prone to exaggeration, so I am intentionally being conservative here in telling you about my flight to freedom where I discovered this oasis.

It all began, after 30 years of marriage when my X (RC) gave me two weeks to move my belongings from our house so his Texas Trash Tramp could move in. You may have discovered that in the middle of a crisis, you just don't think rationally. So, don't even start wondering why I evacuated on demand. I have exactly no idea. I just mindlessly moved out.

All I know (because I still had a key) is that she had nothing to move into my home except suitcases full of very expensive clothing, makeup, and shoes. No blender, no books, not even a wine glass or potato-smasher. I took my potato-smasher by the way. It seemed logical at the time. She got my RC, but she didn't get my potato-smasher or my favorite wine glass!

She did acquire my new furniture and old stained linens. Good for her. I'd like to high-five her with a 2x4 in the face—but I digress. For karma, I left her my mom's hidden ashes for a few weeks. Mom had to be just as pissed as my dog was about that skank squatting in my homestead.

Anyway, I boarded the plane and aimlessly pushed my way to the very back. You know, the seat that doesn't recline. Like most things these days, that seat was not my choice. But it wasn't so bad. I am an optimist. I sat for 149 minutes as they repaired the ventilation system, and it gave me time to ponder why and when they banned potato-smashers in carry-on.

The stale air was suffocating. But overwhelming discomfort came from the fact that the woman in front of me was accompanied by her feline in a carry-on, and I am deathly allergic to cats. Consequently, the moment I squeezed into my corner seat; I was clawing at my swollen red eyes. Luckily, I was distracted by a screaming 4-year-old with a limited vocabulary of "*No*" and "*Stupid.*" His poor mother must have been nearly deaf because that child had to shriek his insults mere inches from her unresponsive face.

We finally pulled away from the gate ... and were delayed ... again.

In my glorious optimism, I controlled the urge to run for an exit. I had just sweated through a 2 ½ hour delay at 98 degrees on blazing asphalt. I knew I could endure another hour going nowhere. Air was finally circulating.

I was squished into my little corner by a couple who loudly popped the gum in their jowls from the moment they sat down, relentlessly swirling their tongues to readjust their globs, efficiently cracking and snapping. I gagged when the passenger in front of me leaned her seat back into my lap (she and her cat).

Finally in the air, I began to breathe easier. Well, until my new friend repeatedly leaned over my body to photograph the clouds commenting on "how close we were to heaven." Meanwhile, her relentless gum popping made me feel like I was in hell!

I suddenly became severely claustrophobic and popped from my seat, escaping to the aisle in one swift leap. It was one of those moves you look back on in amazement. Really, how did I do that?

I stepped into the galley and ordered wine. The flight attendants had observed my "situation" and offered free wine to compensate for my misery. I hung with the flight team for a while, until the conversation turned from my absurd dilemma to airline schedules and crew rosters. Wearing out my welcome, I slyly slipped away.

Not wanting to return to half of my seat, and thinking I had exhausted all options, I haphazardly stumbled upon the most amazing discovery! There just so happen to be private cabins available on airplanes. I know, you didn't know, right?

As many times as I have flown, I never knew about this hidden compartment. You can't book it in advance. It isn't even in first class; it is better, truly private. No one can see you. You can pick your nose without being observed, stand up, move around, sit back, and breathe your own air.

I acquired another complimentary glass of wine, a bag of pretzels, and slithered into the last available secret cabin on the plane without being noticed. It was heavenly. I leaned back on my seat, locked in with my book and wine. It couldn't have been any finer.

After only 38 minutes of bliss, and after ignoring the knock for as long as I thought believable, I folded the door back and peeked out. I had been discovered. I cried inwardly. No other place on the plane offered a private sink, disposable seat covers, and sanitary amenities. The flight attendant said, with true compassion, that I simply must return to my assigned seat and buckle my seatbelt.

It turns out, that lavatories don't have them and, when you fly into extreme turbulence, you are required to wear a stupid seat belt.

I'm pretty sure I suddenly became menopausal during the remainder of the flight. My temperature spiked. I broke out into a cold sweat. I became impatient and irritable. My hair began falling out (probably because I was pulling it). I became overly anxious, and I had absolutely no interest in engaging in sex with any of my fellow passengers. That last observation was not uncommon for me in public places, but I still consider my lack of libido during this flight a valid symptom of my sudden transition to menopause.

Back in the corner, I turned to my seatmate, focused on her mouth, and wondered how much gum they allow in carry-on anyway. Could someone use gum, instead of a potato-smasher, as a weapon? She made much more noise with her gum than I've ever made with my potato-smasher.

When the plane started flying horizontally forward again, passengers removed their seatbelts and discovered the secret cabin. They swarmed in droves toward my utopia, and I never got back in. I had cat dander; the "Stupid" screaming "No" boy; gum-popping; and the tune "Heaven" in my head until we landed…

> Lord help me get away
> From this misery
> How far is heaven
> I know I need to change (seats)
> This ain't livin'
> This ain't heaven.

I optimistically decided that the rest of my flight was an opportune time to plan ahead. I jotted down the following trendsetting turbulent travel coping techniques. (That's quite a mouthful isn't it!)

The first thing I vow to do on my next flight before I even take my seat, is to put a sign on the lavatory door that says, "Do Not Enter." (It's my escape pod) … And I *Will* DOiT.

Travel Sanity
Life-Back-DOiT

Here is your first Life-Back-DOiT Darlin.'

May this, and subsequent DOiTs at the end of each chapter inspire you with uncommon knowledge and skillful mastery of your joyous journeys through the remainder of your life.

On your next flight, if you're allergic to the pet in front of you: slyly bark or meow occasionally. There's really no purpose for this, but I can tell you from experience that it does make time pass more quickly.

If your seat neighbors are annoying, laugh hysterically for five seconds, stop, then glare at them. I guarantee they will stop popping their gum, for a fleeting moment anyway.

The following is a list of essential items to include in your carry-on should you (or I ever) fly again. I believe in sharing, unlike some seat-hogging passengers, and am happy to share these suggestions for your very own…

Travel Sanity Kit:

* Your special wine glass – When you're in cabin seating (economy) you just get a little wine bottle and plastic cup sans stem. If you chose only one item for your carry-on, a magnificent wine glass is fundamental.

* Ear Plugs, or ear pods for your iPod or cassette player (depending on your level of technological evolution).

* Writing pad & pen – so you can document your misery like I did. You can at least start revising your Will in case you decide to jump out of the plane. You could tweet or Facebook it, but years from now when you read it in your notebook—made of paper—you'll LOL louder. Paper never loses power.

* Paper Airplane – to target a loud-mouth brat in the back of the head after the 17th time he screams "NO STUPID" at his apathetic mother. That shouldn't get you in too much trouble if you're not discovered. Besides, it's an effective stress reliever, and really fun.

* Chewing Gum – Not for keeping your ears clear during take-off & landing, but for revenge should my "friends" someday sit by you! It may keep you from chewing *them* out by sharing the joy of annoying activity. Practice now; stick with it, and have a smacking gum time becoming a pop star.
PTSD Warning: If you sit by me while popping your gum, I will straddle your lap and slap you repeatedly.

* Toothbrush – You'll need it since your luggage won't arrive for two days. Plus, if you shelter in the private cabin, heck, you have a sink; so why not erase the evidence of a mediocre Merlot.

* Potato-Smasher – Just for the stimulating conversation and confusion you'll provoke when security pulls it from your firm grasp. I'm still wondering what heinous crimes they imagined me committing with a basic kitchen utensil. Still, I'd rather buy three than leave one for the slut who took over my kitchen. If you are insecure about slipping by TSA with your Potato-Smasher, bring a second one and hide them in boots as boot shapers … odd shape, but it's likely they'll let your Potato-Smashers past security. It's all in the presentation.

So, check-in early (so you can hurry to wait), and find joy in knowing they don't sell gum or serve meals in economy anymore. If you anticipate the likely half-day delay, you may want to consider the following make-ahead snack kit.

The COVID Mask trauma unexplainably caused travelers to become aggressive. To express your frustrations passively, use my Snack Tactics to avoid being banned from commercial jets.

Airplane Snacks for Savory Retribution to Obnoxious Passengers:

* Potato chips in a crinkly bag. Once it's quiet on the plane, open the bag, and eat one at a time, searching diligently for each chip.

* A tiny shampoo bottle (and a conditioner bottle, and lotion bottle) filled with your favorite wine. You brought your favorite wine glass; put it to good use. (Wash the bottles first.)

* An apple & carrots. Make a big crunch and chew with your mouth open to allow the juices to spurt.

* Big whole pickles. Snap off a chunk so that pieces go flying with vinegary spittle.

* Cooked spaghetti. You know how many slurping sounds you can make with long spaghetti!

I learned these food ideas from previous flights. Thank you, fellow passengers, for the inspiration.

Without intending to seem paranoid, I feel compelled to warn you to never, ever, wear an eye mask. Unless, of course, you have a private compartment. No passenger on your flight has your best interests in mind. While you may not want to, you need to be focused on your surroundings. Keep your eyes open for opportunities to lock yourself in the bathroom for the entire flight. Don't forget to put a CLOSED sign on the door. Obviously.

What?

There's nothing wrong with that. There's usually more than one.

Start Your...

DOiT Journal

Sometimes unescapable distractions force you to focus on a better plan. Start by answering these questions:

* Do you have a stressful situation you'd like to escape?

* What is it?

* How can you escape it? (Like, skip backward to get away. Have fun with it.)

* What's something annoying you'd enjoy sharing with the tramp who invaded your life?

* How many ways can you use a Potato-Smasher? Respond to my blog at www.lifebackdoit.com/blog/ with your ideas!

While you read, every time you find an encouraging word you want to remember, write it on a piece of paper & hang it from your smasher with twine or yarn.

Some Potato-Smasher-Words from this chapter:

Virtuous, Mecca, Happy, Ingenious, Paradise, Freedom, Oasis, Shoes, Optimistic, Heaven, Amazing, Complimentary, Compassion, Utopia, LOL, Sharing, Wine.

We'll find even better words in the following chapters. We're just getting started, so grab words as you go and make a feel-good list. I intentionally leave some for you to find, so you can choose freely - like you're going to do with everything else in your life from now on.

2

How to Become a Legend in Your Own Lifetime

"Some people would rather die in their pride than live in their humility"
~Anthony Liccione

Does the thought of being forgotten scare you as much as the possibility of catching an African Sleeping Sickness? It's natural to let your mind wander irrationally when you think you may die of solitude. Becoming suddenly single can petrify you if you don't get your act together. Let me guide you through some concepts to enhance your life and legacy before, well … before you are gone, or forgotten.

Learn to find joy in the fact that you were born alone, and you will die alone. Okay, that's not a joyful thought. But keep reading. You will become wondrously celebrated in this lifetime by using the ideas I've shared.

Finding yourself alone gives you freedom for creative reflection. Silence is easy to hear. You need space to live more purposefully. A good old-fashioned void allows your mind to detox, and you can only do that by yourself.

On my first night alone, I wasn't prepared for what might happen should it get dark in my newly built cabin in the woods. I had forgotten that the sun disappears every night, and I hadn't covered my windows. This allowed a lewd pervert free access to peer at me throughout the night. I had no escape, and the darker it grew, the more terrified I became.

Our divorce agreement awarded me the cabin, the one we planned from the time we met. He got our house in Northern Virginia where his latest slut girlfriend, her daughter, and three granddaughters dictate his life. I've heard she's stupid, younger, scrawny skinny (with fake boobs), and is lactose intolerant. While sounding cruel, I must admit that the miserable life he is living simply makes me so giddy I sometimes wiggle out a little interpretive dance about it.

In contrast to his saturated life, I live alone in my mountain cabin secluded on 15 wooded acres, overlooking the lake. Sounds alluring, doesn't it? But living by myself for the first time, especially at night in the middle of nowhere, was simply horrifying. My brain knew I needed sleep and responded with— may I offer you some irrational fears about perverts in the woods? Or how about a selection of bad memories from the past 10 years?

Obviously, I couldn't sleep in the bed. That's the first place an attacker looks. Besides, I had no idea which box annexed my sheets. So, I pulled a huge bean bag up the stairs into the kitchen. It was the only room with just one window.

I turned on all the lights and gathered my weapons, then realized the prowlers could see me, so I turned off the lights. I plopped myself down between open cabinet doors, in the safety of darkness, with my flashlight and steak knife. Pulling a blanket to my chin, I wrapped the end of it around my head so that only my eyes and nose were visible to creeps lurking outside the kitchen window. My thumb was ready on the car panic button so the coyotes could hear my alarm when the outsiders finally got in. My nearest neighbor was a mile away through the unpaved woods.

It occurred to me that I could have gone upstairs for safety, but I was already frozen in place, hiding from danger. Besides, murderers could have already broken in and staged their attack from the loft, waiting for me to fall asleep. That wasn't going to happen. I was rigid and ready, staring at the ceiling, listening to them creaking across the floor. I lay firm on my beanbag, not budging, barely breathing, poised for action as the cracking turbulence grew louder.

By 3:52 am, I was considering duct tape for the stove's glowing clock which doubled as an eyeball spotlight.

There are 62 brown knots in the wood on my kitchen ceiling. Some are natural defects where tree limbs had grown from the trunk. Nineteen other wood markings are clearly peering faces, eerie creatures, and dangerous animals. By 4:48 am, some of them began gesturing and moving around, making intimidating faces, mocking my paranoia.

I really had to pee. But I knew that if I were to get up before sunlight, it was an irresistible invitation for strangers to enter my fort. The creaking grew louder as the night wore on. Edgar Allan Poe was in my head "Harken! and observe how healthily how calmly I can tell you the whole story."

The next day, I unpacked boxes and prepared for my second night in the cabin. I hung a tarp over the kitchen window, added a hammer to my defense weaponry, covered the glowing stove clock, and settled in before dusk. Having not slept the night before, I was sure to quickly fall asleep with a well-equipped arsenal on my chest and my glass of wine just under the open sink cabinets by the beanbag.

Why hadn't I noticed last night how brightly the smoke detector light beamed down on me?

At 2:22 am, I considered shining my flashlight at the window to scare the faint shadow that slowly moved outside the window over my sink. But then what would I do to him, throw the hammer through the window? Undoubtedly, he could see me with the smoke detector glowing on my face.

As I switched the car alarm to my other thumb, I heard the familiar squeaky wood upstairs. He began moving more confidently around the house, knowing I was truly alone. His accomplices shamelessly threw twigs onto the tin roof to frighten and distract me. But I stayed right where I was, flat (in the beanbag) on my back, keenly aware of every maddening clunk throughout the night.

On the third day, secluded in the mountains, I shared my dilemma with knowing friends. Guess what, the creaking and cracking all over my cabin was what THEY call "settling." Also, the change in temperature from day to night causes contraction and expansion in the logs and tin roof. The moving shadow outside my window went away when my son responded to my emergency call and removed the flag from my flagpole.

So why hadn't all that noise scared away the perpetrator? He couldn't have known that the *tell-tale* noises were Mother Nature putting my house in place. I was convinced that he could still hear my heart beating louder … louder … (I don't even like Edgar Allan Poe, but his words haunted my thoughts.)

On my fourth and fifth nights alone in the dark and dangerous cabin in the woods, I made incredible progress. I was still scared stiff, (attempting to sleep) on the kitchen floor with one eye open.

Bonus Info: Dolphins actually sleep with one eye open. Just like dolphins in the ocean, I had nowhere else to go. So, I went with the flow. I was pretty sure I wasn't going to die (well, everyone dies). But I needed to get on with living. Not everyone does *that*, you know: Really Live. We're going to DOiT now.

While loading the dishwasher, I encountered nothing but coffee cups and wine glasses. Their contents had kept me alive those first few days. The wine glasses made me feel elegantly indulged. Spoiling myself with a good wine in a fabulous wine glass from time to time is even better than a unique assortment of potato-smashers.

My coffee cup collection reveals random vacations, attractions, and status updates. I'm the World's Best Mama, Friend, and Daughter. Coffee keeps me busy until it's time to drink wine, and "I have 'pour judgment'… there may be wine in my mug" (according to the cups). I remember who gave me every glorious wine glass or coffee cup. Wine is wonderful, but I do love my coffee.

Have you ever wondered why people call it MY coffee or YOUR coffee? No one just drinks THE coffee.

I've watched people grasp their coffee cup with both hands as if I were going to grab it or sneak a slurp of their coffee if they looked away. Why would I do that when I'd already poured MY coffee?

I know I'm off subject but, people do that with showers too. Isn't it obvious who's shower you take? "I took My shower." Go take Your shower. No, I want to take Your shower; you take My bath while I sneak a drink of Your coffee.

By the third cup of coffee, it's time for a glass of wine anyway. Which reminds me, I did make a culinary drink-pairing discovery. Let's call it a drinkery revelation: If you are busy on the computer or reading or writing, and you have both leftover wine and coffee in front of you, you likely pick up one or the other without paying attention to your selection.

If you mistakenly take a sip of Your coffee when you prefer the wine … well then, just immediately take a sip of wine. It turns out that coffee chased by wine, and vice versa, creates quite a pleasant mouth party. It's a marvelous way to keep your palate entertained!

It's amazing what you discover when left unattended in your own head with countless hours of seclusion and fatigue to console your unanticipated desolation. I don't even know what that means. I'm just tired.

After eleven days of solitude, I learned that RC had actually *married* that trashy tramp he boinked for the last two years of our marriage. It was late in the evening when I read the enlightening email from a former co-worker. I immediately called my boys; two of them were also in the dark. The third just didn't want to tell me.

"Anger" is a fluffy description of my reaction. I realized I simply wasn't afraid anymore. I was furious. I was shocked, outraged, livid, and cursing aloud. (Not good Potato-Smasher-Words.)

Inspirited by a bottle of wine, I turned on all the lights and yelled to all the creepy lurkers inside and out, every criminal, spirit, ghost, intruder, and entity … informing them, at the top of my lungs, that this was *my* cabin, and I was in control. I took possession (undoubtedly appearing to be possessed), vowing to never be afraid of anything again. I slept in my bed that night, with new shades and my steak knives in the kitchen drawer. I didn't even hear the wood or tin roof cooling down for the night.

What was I afraid of anyway? The chipmunks were asleep. The raccoons and bears had already shown more interest in the trash bins than getting inside the cabin. The deer just wanted my azaleas. No one could find me on GPS, so my would-be attackers were probably elsewhere … somewhere with a driveway that didn't require a 4x4 to ascend. If they had chosen to hike in, villains would be too exhausted by the time they climbed the driveway to do me any harm.

Besides, if they were looking in my windows that night, they'd have been much more afraid than I have ever been! I was crying, screaming, and flailing around the cabin like a rodeo clown.

That was the first night I had prayed for the past few years.
I prayed to die. How ironic. I just spent the last two weeks posing myself to avoid death. In my hysteria, that somehow seemed funny. I started imagining what it would be like if I did die. My family would be sad. My friends would say I checked out too soon, and all of them

would compete to tell the most outrageous, unbelievable story about my misadventures until they were old and senile, laughing themselves to death.

What would be even funnier is if I faked my death and haunted RC and that Opportunist Pampered Falsified Shameless Shallow Slut who stole my marriage. So, I devised a plan. I knew that faking my own death would be a lot of work, and probably not tax-deductible. But the benefits far outweighed the alternative ... living with the fact that he really did marry that Stupid Shallow Phony Texas Trash Tramp. Yes, I'd have the last laugh.

I realized that being dead meant I'd soon be forgotten, and never be invited to another pool party or class reunion. On the other hand, I'd have instant gratification and temporary acclaim. The dearly departed are immediately bestowed the halo effect. Seriously, how often does anyone stand up at a funeral to talk about annoying habits or the useless life of the passed soul? I'd be suddenly magnificent in every way!

Of course, I would attend my own funeral disguised as a beautiful young and admiring woman. (There's no way I'd miss my first funeral.) All I could think was: He had better be there! I'd hire professional mourners to wail and faint. I'd write my very own glorified eulogy, praising my idolized life. Then I'd put together a video presentation of my most flattering photos and VCR recordings, especially the ones of him with me (just in case *she* had the audacity to show up).

Naturally, I'd hire a juggler for the ceremony since everyone knows how I unsuccessfully practice the respected art of juggling. Maybe a fire baton twirler at the gravesite would be a dazzling finish since I was a majorette! Symbolic and meaningful tributes to my life danced through my head with gruesome delight.

Death suddenly became an idea I could live with. I knew I'd have to be convincing. My death must look authentic, as if one of those elusive murderers finally broke into the cabin, slashed the beanbag, threw the hammer out the window, and took my body with him. That isn't very sexy, but the best I could come up with in my excited state of fake post-mortem bliss.

Feeling more motivated as the night wore on (I was still sleep-deprived), I imagined the steps I'd take. I became intoxicated with the thought … me, dead, taking steps. That would scare RC. He would undoubtedly develop a severe case of morbophobia when my plan played out.

Can you believe there's no such word as morbophobia? THEY call fear of death Thanatophobia, and fear of dead things Necrophobia. Regardless, RC's forecasted phobia of me (dead) shall be declared – Morbophobia. It just has a nice ring to it. THEY claim a phobia for everything these days, and I deserve a memorial phobia. Besides, I like inventing words. And I digress.

My first task in faking my death would be to arrange the crime scene. First, I'd fill the bathtub with red food coloring. Wearing full-body (slimming) Spanx, socks, and gloves, I'd immerse myself until completely soaked, head to toe.

Then I'd lie on a large white rug with one arm above my head and the opposite leg kicked out behind me. I'd strip off my swathing and trace the devastatingly flattering outline of my body with some colorful chalk. Note to self: Get dressed before leaving the crime scene.

Second step: Leave a ransom note stipulating where to send massive amounts of money to recover my body. It seemed likely that he may not be terribly interested in recovering my body … even though he used to appreciate it.

The murder note would say, "I have killed her. Send money and alimony to her Go Fund Me account. Don't even think you will find the body; there never was one quite like hers.

Signed: The Crazy Murderer who finally broke into the cabin."

Lastly, I'd grim-reap the benefits. How rousing to show up at his wedding anniversary parties. At some point, he'd be in the early stages of dementia and be insanely confused by seeing a somewhat familiar face dancing on the table in the back corner of the ballroom.

I could enjoy a life of tormenting them by walking past their house at night—shining a flashlight up my nose. I'd dedicate songs like "Stayin' Alive" and "I'll Sleep When I'm Dead" to him on the radio, making sure they included my voice in the broadcast request.

I would send him (and his trash-tramp wife-slut) Christmas cards from heaven every year with a newsletter applauding my splendors. Flattering photos of me—with his new car and unnecessarily huge house in the background—would be an arousing visual. Glitter would spill from the envelope (and *Someone* would have to clean it up).

The only disadvantage would be that I couldn't go back to the cabin for the monumental buffet and party after my funeral. But at least I'd have the best selection of houseplants and flowers. They were intended for me, so I could justifiably take them from the gravesite without remorse.

It would be considerate of me to participate in the notability of my funeral gathering by sending cordial gifts and food. Lifesize cutouts of me in varying poses (trimmed down) would ensure that my funeral party was festive and memorable. James Dean said, "Dream as if you'll live forever; live as if you'll die today."

You really should consider the celebration of your life while you're still alive. Do it now, or do it for … you know, when you're not here to do it. Now is a good time to plan your Life Celebration and Get Your Life-Back-DOiT!

Keep on Living your
Life-Back-DOiT

When preparing your fake funeral, be thoughtful at a time like this and contribute to your own celebration. Become legendary, admirable, and memorable before you (actually) die.

* Send disposable plates and toilet paper with your photo on them (of course "disposable" toilet paper)
* Leave freezer bags and containers (you can sneak in later to retrieve leftovers)
* Provide heavy-duty garbage bags (Open the box and take one, as if it were used for your body bag)

Comfort Food with a Higher Calling for your Plan-ahead Funeral Gathering:

The tradition of funeral food is about spending time with family and friends, and it's always about eating. In the south, we say "it's potato salad time" when someone dies. That's because everyone takes potato salad to the home of the deceased; it's comfort food. Make extra. Like us, potato salad gets better with age, and we nearly departed deserve extra comfort food at a time like this.

Everyone knows how to make potato salad, and claims theirs to be the very best, so I'm sharing a different good-grief recipe for those of us who aren't too chicken to fake our own death.

Chicken Pot Pie Comfort

(A Bird in the Casserole Dish is Worth Two at your Funeral)

– So, double the recipe and make one for yourself (in case there aren't any leftovers to steal later).

Ingredients

- 4 large boneless chicken breasts
- 1 cup of white wine
- 3 cups of chicken broth
- 3 tbsp. finely chopped fresh parsley
- 1 bay leaf
- 3 tbsp. butter
- 10 cloves of minced garlic
- 1 cup chopped celery
- 3/4 cup chopped carrots
- 2 tbsp. finely minced shallots
- 1 large onion, finely chopped
- 1 cup of sliced mushrooms
- 2 cups of frozen peas
- 3 tbsp. cornstarch
- ¼ cup cream
- ¼ cup whole milk to brush the crust (SHE is lactose intolerant after all)
- Salt & pepper
- A few dashes of Tabasco sauce
- 2 Pie Crusts (the kind you roll out & shape yourself)
- Cayenne Pepper for your X and his wife. Have a trusted friend season it for them with (quite) a few extra tablespoons

Steps

1. Combine the first 6 ingredients in a heavy pan.
2. Poach on low until chicken is tender.
3. Remove the chicken to cool & save the broth.
4. Preheat oven to 350 and pour a glass of good wine into your favorite wine glass.
5. Drink it.
6. Sauté celery, carrots, garlic, shallots, & onions in butter until transparent.
7. Add mushrooms and continue to sauté until tender.

8. Reduce to a simmer, cover, and cook 4 more minutes.
9. In the meantime, have another glass of wine and cut the chicken into small cubes.
10. Roll out the pie crust to line a 9 x 13 casserole dish & up the sides of the pan.
11. Stir in the chicken and peas.
12. Drain ¾ cup of the hot liquid into a small bowl and whisk in cornstarch.
13. Pour into the sauté and stir in cream.
14. Add Tabasco, Salt & pepper. Pour into the crust and top with a second crust.
15. Cut small slits and decorative designs into the top of the crust. A skull and crossbones would work if you can't create your own portrait.
16. Bake for 30 minutes. Finish that bottle of wine.
17. Brush the top of the crust with milk and continue to bake for 5-10 minutes until the crust is golden.

If the jezebel who broke up your marriage will be there and is also lactose-intolerant, use more milk than usual, and hide the toilet paper.

Have the casserole delivered by someone in a Big Bird costume to liven things up. You never want your post-funeral get-together to be dull. This will turn conversations from stolen funeral flowers to "what in heaven's name was that?"

Since I can't openly attend my family gathering, I plan to grab a few of the pre-saved leftovers and hide outside in the bushes to eat, stealing glimpses of my loved ones through the windows, while trying to award a glimpse of myself to RC's trash tramp. If my plan works, and she alone sees and confronts me, I'll simply smile and say, "You can *SEE* me?" as I back away before anyone else does.

DOiT Journal.

What do you want to do before you die?

When are you going to DOiT? (Not die, when are you going to do those things you want to do *before* you go?)

What songs, verses, stories, and photos do you want at your funeral?

(Write 'em down now, before, you know, you can't.)

Potato-Smasher-Words:

Joyful, Celebrated, Giddy, Alluring, Safety, Glow, Progress, Live, Fabulous, Coffee, Glorious, Wonderful, Pleasant, Enlightening, Admiring, Juggling, Dazzling, Sexy, Flattering, Splendorous, Glitter, Cordial, Thoughtful, Magnificent, Comfort, Considerate, Festive, Memorable, Legendary, Wine, Wiggle...

Ok, I got carried away, so I'm leaving out more words (for you to find) in the following chapters. Start choosing words you want. Start choosing how you want words to make you feel. Don't the encouraging words feel good?

Write 'em down & hang them from your Potato-Smasher!

3

A Good Reason to
Wear Underwear

*"Do you wish to rise? Begin by descending. You plan a tower
that will pierce the clouds? Lay first the foundation of humility."*
~St. Augustine

When you feel cut off from the rest of the world, you may feel like your
heart has been stripped from you.

It can seem like a bottomless pit of emptiness. Solitaire is a sad game to
play (although we do, don't we) and it's more challenging when the 2-of-
hearts is missing. The phase between a broken heart and finding yourself
again is probably the most difficult. It's like being helplessly naked and alone.
I hate it when that happens. But it does.

Every Autumn, my Appalachian Mountain cabin is surrounded by bright
happy color. Consequently, my decks are adorned with mounds of fallen
leaves. A big storm was brewing one lonely Monday afternoon, so I
scrambled to get the leaves cleared before it rained. I rushed upstairs to the
loft and out onto my top deck, 26 feet above the flower garden.

I know from experience, that sweeping a pile of heavy soaked leaves is
akin to combing tangled wet hair with a toothbrush. I was determined to beat
the cloudburst. But the rain was pounding before I even got started.

The crazy wind slammed the door behind me.

Time stopped. I turned and stared at the locked door. There were no stairs to the ground. All I had was a broom and a glass of Merlot.

Standing on the balcony, I looked around, wondering what to do next. Drink wine, of course. As the rain beat down on me, my first thought was "normally I would escape on my broom." Gushing at my own good humor, I finished my rain-diluted wine, waiting for an epiphany.

I was beginning to feel like Dorothy in Kansas as tree limbs went flying and black skies overtook the afternoon. My festive fall scarecrow had blown over onto the haystack, and if I had a tin man he'd be rusted in place by now. I felt corroded and cowardly on the deck, wishing I had some flying monkeys to rescue me.

After the novelty of my Oz fantasy wore off, I started thinking ... it would be a week before anyone dropped by the cabin. I knew I couldn't just stand there, amusing myself alone, in the chilling rain.

"I am really alone now!" I yelled into the tempest as I yanked on the doorknob with both hands. I had been ignoring the fact that my life had permanently become void of a partner. There was simply no chance of a rescue any time soon. What other slapdash plans could I possibly come up with to find my way back into the cabin?

Motivated by the dropping temperature and my drippy attire, absurd ideas for making a break without breaking something swept through my windblown head. But I had no ladder, no phone, and no parachute.

My cabin is invisible from the road, so I couldn't signal for help. I entertained the thought of jumping into the koi pond below. Surely, I could make it. The water would be frigid, yet warmer than a chilling rainstorm. Then again, the pond was only four feet deep—and slimy. Besides, that bubbling fountain would have been extremely unpleasant to land on. The thought of a painful plunge enhanced my chills.

I suddenly became more analytical and less comical as lightning flashed near the pond. I was temporarily glad to be trapped on the balcony rather than freed and fried in the pond. A stroke of brilliance overtook me, and I decided to throw my Adirondack chairs down, strategically stacking them on top of each other. I skillfully did so, and … and, then the chairs were on the ground, far below my reach. Great. I had nothing to sit on as I shivered in the storm. For some reason, I had imagined that last idea to be a good start to a plan of some sort.

But it wasn't.

If I had a credit card with me, I thought, I could slide the card between the doors to effortlessly unlatch the locks like detectives (or thieves) do. But I failed to take my credit cards with me to sweep the upper deck. I gave myself no grief about forgetting the plastic and moved on to my next brilliant strategy.

Milling over my prospects, I recalled that people sometimes tied their sheets together to escape a burning building, but dang, I had neglected to grab sheets on my way out. There they were, on the bed, just inside the locked double doors. I pressed my hands and face to the glass, but couldn't think of a way to get to them. I was running out of ideas.

Motivated to get out of my soaking jeans and T-shirt anyway, I took them off, tied them together, and hung them from the bottom of the railing. I should really start wearing underwear.

Luckily my dad taught me to sail and tie knots, and I learned rappelling at Boy Scout mother/son day a few years back. I was confident that I could slither down the side of my cabin. Well, maybe I was feeling more desperate than confident, but I had exhausted all possibilities.

The most frightening stunt was climbing over the railing. I promptly recognized, as I straddled the rail cap, that I needed to get over the safety of my perch and somehow down to my clothes from there. Then I realized that the probability of someone just happening by the cabin was very high, as I clung to the top banister in the pouring rain, naked.

That was all the incentive I needed to move.

During my descent, I imagined what would happen if my knots didn't hold or I lost my grip. I would be found naked on the ground, with my clothing tied to the balcony. At my funeral, my sons would be sitting there together as the minister began: "They put her clothes back on and re-attached her legs." My boys would fall into a fit of laughter, with recurrent episodes throughout the day. The thought of giving them another reason to laugh at me (at my second funeral) was my courage to continue.

My scouting skills came into play as I wrapped my legs around my clothing & shimmied on down, landing in my huge rhododendron bushes. When I safely reached solid ground, I ran for the back door. It was locked. The front door was locked, as were the basement, and my bedroom doors. No windows were unlatched. I was still locked out, bare-skinned, getting very clean, feeling very green. I've always liked being naked outside, but it could have been more fun.

I stood there as the rain washed over my (newly-bruised, bleeding) arms hanging by my sides. I must have looked crazy a few minutes ago, running around au-naturelle, trying all the doors and windows, cursing at each one. I am not making this story up. Believe me, I'm not that imaginative. Hopefully, no one was lurking in the woods. I'm always worried about that.

I may have been misleading though; I wasn't completely nude. I was still wearing socks and a tennis shoe (I lost a shoe in the bushes). That left me with a smither of dignity until I remembered that Murphy's Law dictated my life, and someone was sure to stop by any minute to witness me running around in the rain like it was my birthday. It's hard, in the beginning, not to imagine that someone will rescue you, no matter how forbidding the circumstances may be.

I began laughing so hard I cried. Or maybe I cried so hard it felt like laughing. In any event, I knew it would be a welcome respite to be locked away in a dry, safe little padded room for a few years. I sort of hoped someone would come by after all.

My mind caught up, and the idea of someone finding me in that condition propelled me into action again. I ran to the garage and punched the code to enter. Then, I spent another 25 minutes searching for that extra key I had so cleverly hidden for a situation nothing like this. I just couldn't remember where that strategic hiding-place was, so I found my stash of favorite wines, picked up a bottle, and there it was! Who doesn't hide an extra key under a random bottle of wine?

Naturally, the only key I found was the key to the upstairs balcony. REALLY? My sense of humor was lost in the fog. But at least it had stopped raining.

I knew I didn't have the strength to pull myself back up my jeans and T-shirt onto the balcony. But after a little more time outside in my socks and shoe, as the temperature continued to drop, I chose to try climbing back up to the balcony rather than break a window. So, I stood up on the bottom porch railing and grabbed a leg of my jeans.

I knew this wasn't a good idea, and apparently so did my guardian angel. Lo and behold, from the clearing sky, and from the pocket of my jeans, my front-door key fell to the ground. I didn't even want to know if my credit card was in the back pocket of my jeans.

This was more discomforting than finding my misplaced toothbrush in the freezer. As I unlocked my front door, I began searching for my favorite crystal wine glass and wondered if a frozen toothbrush would comb wet hair more effortlessly than a wet toothbrush. There was no telling where my comb was.

You too may benefit someday by knowing how to tie secure knots with your clothing. It's much easier to use a rope. But whatever you tie, here are some gripping knots that may get you out of a bind someday. Just check your pockets for better ideas before you drop your pants. It's Knot like you can't DOiT.

A Somewhat Twisted
Life-Back-DOiT

Knot Know-How

Bowline

The bowline has been called the king of knots. It will never slip or jam if properly made and, thus, is excellent for tying around a person in a rescue. When rescuing yourself from a balcony, pull your pant legs apart for a longer reach.

Begin by forming a loop with one end (the bottom of a leg of your jeans). Then take the other leg up through the loop, around the banister (standing part), and back where it came from - down through the loop.

This is the knot you may have learned using a bunny journey: Up through the rabbit hole, round the big tree; down through the rabbit hole, and off goes he.

Bonus: This knot can be tied with one hand - in case you have a wine glass in the other.

Half Hitch

The half hitch is the start of several other hitches and is useful all by itself as a temporary attaching knot. It will hold against a steady pull. Wrap one jeans leg under the banister and hold your jeans in the air. Pass the rest of your jeans around the standing portion and back under the loop.

The half hitch is more suitable for tying clothing to your balcony than most other knots (unless you're wearing silk pants, then you're just screwed).

Sailor's Knot

The sailor's knot is basically two half hitches. Pulling the knot back along the line, it goes around and can be used to make the line taut. This may be a little safer than the half hitch if you've recently put on a few pounds.

Lariat Loop

This knot forms a fixed loop through which a cowgirl pokes the remaining long rope to form a hoop. She spins the hoop overhead holding the long rope (lots of wrist action), and throws it to lasso an animal or a very handsome man (sometimes you can't tell the difference). You may find this knot handy once you escape a balcony or a bad relationship. Use a rope.

Square Knot

You may already know how to tie a square knot. It's the first step when tying your shoes. First, right over left and twist. Then left over right and twist. You can loosen the square knot easily by either pushing the ends toward the knot or by "upsetting" the knot by pulling back on one end and pulling the other through the loops.

The square knot is also called a reef knot because it is used by sailors to 'reef' or shorten sails in bad weather or to secure sails when in port. It ties flat, so it doesn't scrape your naked thighs.

Sheet Bend

The sheet bend is the most important knot for joining two rope ends, especially if the ropes are different sizes (as in T-shirt and jeans). Sailors named it in the days of sailing ships when they would "bend" (tie) the "sheets"(ropes) attached to the clew of the sail.

Form a loop in one end of your jeans. Pass the free end of your T-shirt under the opening of the loop, around both ends of the jeans leg below the loop, and back under itself (the shirt).

Pull all four ends to tighten.

Two wraps around both parts of the jeans make a Doubled Sheet Bend.

Snug it carefully before applying any bodyweight to the knot.

Now, practice taking your clothes off in a seductive way. You don't have to tie them together, but you may as well have some fun.

DOiT Journal.

If you were Dorothy in the Wizard of Oz, with three dudes, and needed to sacrifice your clothing for an escape, would you take your shirt off, or take your jeans off first?

What inspires you to remove your clothing anyway?

What have you done to rescue yourself?

What made you laugh today?

Potato-Smasher-Words:

Bright, Happy, Merlot, Good, Humor, Laughter, Amazing, Comical, Glad, Confident, Nude, Sailor, Fun.
Add some of your own.

I've saved the best for last.

4

Dancing Nightmare

"Mastery beings with humility"
~Robin Sharma

Did you know that nightmares are not necessarily a bad thing?

THEY say nightmares are your brain's way of tackling stress, fear, and anger. We may tackle them, but anger and aggression are sometimes still in the game, teamed up with disappointment, heartbreak, uncertainty, and some comforting bitterness. Maneuvering through unconscious delusions in your sleep may reveal that your defensive mood has become "pissed off."

You can decide to change your defensive mood and take the offense, now. Make it your goal to replace nightmares and bad memories with dreams. Make it your dream to stop having nightmares! To do so, think happy thoughts before you go to sleep. Think about Peter Pan or cotton candy. Slide something into your noggin that takes your mind to a dreamy place and charms you.

After divorce, although I've always enjoyed being naked outdoors, I nonetheless had nightmares that I was naked, alone, and homeless. It was a terrible illusion that could have been brought on by leaving my career, moving to the cabin, and moving out periodically to rent to vacationers. I offered my cabin as a vacation rental to compensate for not having a traditional job.

The injustice of divorce is that one person must move out. I don't recall how it was decided that I was the one who should be uprooted from home and career, but here I am in the cabin, 262 miles from my last paying job. It is a beautiful, secluded hideaway, nestled in the mountains of Virginia. It's so far from reality that I call it Lost Horizon.

The trouble with living in a hidden utopia is that there are simply no career choices.

Ok, "no career choices" isn't truly definitive. Walmart is only 12 miles away, next to McDonalds. While there may be an opportunity there, I'd surely spend more on gas than I'd make greeting and directing people to the candy clearance aisle or encouraging someone to add fries to their order.

I needed something a little more challenging, like organizing wine festivals, or writing government proposals for military invasion support; maybe training the FBI on using a database to find criminals … stuff I have experience in.

Since the local convenience stores didn't offer those positions, I got creative to make ends meet. I rented my cabin to city folk and various other foreigners as a weekend vacation retreat. Lost Horizon is my gift to visitors who want some hiking, biking, water sports, and relaxation in a luxurious Shangri-La to escape civilization.

So, for a few hundred dollars, a few weekends a month, I moved my belongings into the garage, grabbed the eternally packed suitcase, and headed down to my camper on the lakefront (hidden by a privacy fence behind the bonfire pit). It was less than ideal. The camper had no running water or septic, just a hose from the neighbor's well and a sewage holding tank that I dumped into my septic system up at the cabin. Talk about humility, or is that humiliation?

When in the camper, I was held hostage by cabin guests on the dock. I parked my car behind a little shed and kept all noise and motion to a minimum to accommodate the guests who owned my property that week.

Not that I usually pumped up the hip-hop and danced freely on the porch, but I made a game of not being noticed when families were playing horseshoes or taking my canoes out on the lake.

I didn't want my renters to know I was lurking in the camper. The memorable days were when the temperature was above 95. I had air conditioning but didn't use it when assuming my incognito position. The camper became a free sweatbox, and I could have lost countless pounds of sweat fat. But I didn't; I just stank.

Cleaning out and polishing up *Lost Horizon* gave me a sense of accomplishment and a free workout. I'd start in the loft (sweeping off the balcony—the one you may remember, has no dignified escape route), and continue downstairs. I'd take apart the refrigerator, stove, nightstands, and anything with moving parts.

I methodically arranged all amenities, coffee cups, and wine glasses. Even the fireplaces were immaculate. It took me all day just to move out, then another day to sparkle up the cabin and arrange welcome gifts, soaps, and information pamphlets.

By the time I reached the bottom level, where the bar, wine fridge, laundry room, and steam shower are, I was near the point of collapse. I usually worked my way into the last bathroom, stripped off my clothes, and hopped into the shower for a final scrub-down of both the shower and my *self.*

One memorable day, I jumped out and threw my wet towel & clothes in the storage room, locked it, then ran to get dressed and out of the cabin. I had an hour before the renters were due to arrive. On this banner day, I started a movement in the tourism industry that gave incentive to travelers to adhere to check-in times.

Do you ever have one of those dreams—nightmares, really—where you are at work or in school, naked, panicked, and have nowhere to hide? You are suddenly in a crowd, and you are the only person standing naked in the congregation.

I have proof that dreams do come true. There I was, wide-awake, face-to-face with my renters, stark naked with nowhere to go but past them, up the stairs where I left my change of clothes. I was horrified and paralyzed.

They are still in therapy.

Have you ever passed someone in a narrow hallway, and you both do that little dance ... side to side; the one where neither of you commits to left or right, bobbing back and forth? In a perfect world, you'd say something witty like "wanna dance?" Or you'd both laugh, and someone would take the initiative to pass on the right.

That didn't happen.

I have big boobs. But nothing triggered the natural response in my brain to cover them. No, I started a dance instead ... with my gloriously exposed palms swaying back and forth in their faces, stepping side to side, with everything swinging in rhythm to a song in my head:

> Should I stay or can I go now?
> Oh man, this is trouble.
> But If I stay it will be double.
> I can't think, and I don't know!
> Do I stay or should I go?

All of a sudden, I gave them a view of my full moon, grabbed my wine glass, and ran out the door to my garage where I store extra clothing. I left without explanation, and I'm pretty sure they never came back or communicated with me in any way after that. There wasn't much more to say.

Being exposed to one of my worst nightmares nudged me to share a few dance moves you may find useful the next time you find yourself in a Naked Situation. Anything is probable, and you can DOiT!

Just Dance a little
Life-Back-DOiT

The Moonwalk

I learned the moonwalk as part of my self-guided trauma therapy. It is much smoother than my side-to-side steps that go nowhere. Once you master this move, you can use it to back away gracefully. I suggest practicing the moonwalk wearing socks, on a smooth wood or marble floor, fully clothed. Basketball courts are an ideal surface for learning to dance a disciplined moonwalk. But wait until the game is over.

Also remember, unless you become extremely good at the moonwalk it will be very hard to impress anyone by demonstrating it with or without clothing. So, practice diligently, as this move could be very beneficial the next time you find yourself naked in front of strangers.

1. Start with your feet a little closer together than shoulder width.
2. Align your right foot toes with the middle of your left foot.
3. Lift your right heel and put your weight on your right foot.
4. Now slide the left foot straight back, keeping it flat on the ground, until your left foot's toes are aligned with the middle of the right foot.
5. Next, drop your right heel to the ground and lift your left heel at the same time. This switching part is what makes the moonwalk look slick. The smoother it is, the smoother your groove.
6. Now slide your right foot back until your toes reach the middle of your left foot and switch again.

You may have succumbed to the temptation to get up & do this. Maybe not, but it's really easy. Trust me, it's a skill you'll want to use someday. Do it with pride and confidence. That makes it more impressive.

In conjunction with the moonwalk; it's always entertaining to combine your moves to include the dance move called the "POP."

I call it the arm snake because that's what it looks like. Calling it a "snake" may help to distract from the fact that you are nude—especially if you announce your routine to your viewers while performing.

The Naked Snake Arm Move is a real attention-getter.

Think: shoulder/elbow/wrist/fingertips…

It's really just an alternating shoulder roll with rubbery arms.

1. Roll your right shoulder back & bring your elbow up.
2. Throw your arm in the air leading with your wrist & dangling your fingers. Keep palms down.
3. Flip your fingers upward & let everything fall down thru your wrist, keeping your arms away from your body.
4. Lower your right shoulder as you roll your left shoulder up & back & do the same thing on the other side.

Don't sweat the actual mechanics; Practice competing with one of those car dealership inflatable tube-man wacky wavers. Or imagine scooting your fingers under a big blob of jelly, rolling it from your fingertips across the top of your arm to your shoulder, across the back of your neck to the other shoulder, and down the other arm to your fingertips … and back.

Just snake it out; you know you look good.

For an unforgettable performance, I suggest starting with the moonwalk to create some distance. Follow up with the snake arm pop. Then, if you roll out a little twerking as your finale, your children (or anyone who loves you) will be so proud when you spontaneously demonstrate your moves in front of their friends.

DOiT Journal.

What are your worst nightmares?

Why are they (Not) realistic?

What is the first thing that comes to mind when asked: What is your dream?

What would you like to do, as if dancing like no one were watching?

Potato-Smasher-Words:

Dreams, Beautiful, Encouraging, Luxurious, Wine, Laugh, Dance, Proud, Good, Sparkle, Confidence, Impressive.

5

Dump the Dirt & Indulge

"Humility is throwing oneself away in complete concentration on something or someone else."
~Madeleine L'Engle

Are you still wasting energy digging through your past? Nothing has changed; the past never will. That's a good thing. It gives you a definitive place to start concentrating on your future. Start Here and Now.

Throw yourself into something new. Something good. I know, I know, you have already been thrown into a cringe-worthy existence. Thank the Almighty that nothing lasts forever, and throw yourself into a fit of laughter, or into a single, handsome, virtuous, healthy man. Get creative. If you're thrown in the mud, make a facial mask. I'm serious.

I threw myself into maintaining my cabin. It's a real struggle, attempting maintenance and repair jobs without the slightest indication of ability. The only *handyman* I can afford to hire has skills I don't have and have yet to acquire. Let's face it: most men have a few abilities we don't, and some men are just too expensive. So, I do everything (well lots of things) myself to economize.

It saves plastic and money to haul truckloads of mulch instead of sissy 10-pound bags from the home stores. So, I did. I was unloading a two-scoop heap of mulch from the back of my truck. Sweat trickled down my butt crack as I shoveled the mulch into the wheelbarrow 62 times and wheeled it to different locations.

When I was down to the last of it, creative efficiency was all I had left. I was plum tuckered out. Crawling into the truck for the last time, I pulled the tarp back, baffled by how heavy 8 inches of mulch can be. There didn't seem to be that much mulch left, but at least 5 more wheelbarrow loads were spread in the truck bed. I had no strength to shovel another load.

But it had to be done. So, I mustered my muscle and folded the edges of the tarp until most of it was sequestered into a seemingly manageable pile. Backing out of the truck, pulling my mound, I miscalculated and stepped off the back of the truck, landing on my back with the tarp full of mulch unloaded on top of me in the driveway.

After I regained consciousness, my first delirious thought was … I have fallen and I can't get up! Remember that hilariously dramatic TV commercial?

It's not that funny when you can't breathe. Besides, I absolutely could not get up! (At first.) Ants and spiders were crawling around me, and gravel was digging into my back. I had every reason to wiggle frantically from under the heap and skitter around the yard waggling unthinkable critters from my hair.

The second thought in my jolted head was something I read somewhere. Did you know that turtles can breathe through their butt? A turtle would have suffocated in my predicament. I was glad I wasn't a turtle. Well, most days, I guess, I'm ok with not being a turtle.

My third thought was how *mulch* had changed in my life because of divorce.

When exactly was it that I stopped wearing hose and heels every day?

I flat-out loathed that prissy unemployed ferret-face Texas Trash Tramp who pranced around my former house when she was not busy at the spa or shopping and eating out. I wanted to take all my new fire ants (the ones that came free with the mulch) & dump them in my old yard, (where she lives now) and fantasize about her falling into them. Bitterness is a taste I hadn't planned on acquiring, so I decided right then and there that I'd make my life sweeter.

I realized that I too deserved a spa day, and I'd find a way to afford it. So, after I crawled out of the mulch, I researched and made up a motherload of homemade recipes for an indulgent pampering ritual. Get prepared for Goddess Day girls.

Get your favorite wine glass (and put something wonderful in it). Light a few candles. Play some Barry Manilow, Frank Sinatra, Michael Bublé, or smooth jazz.

Whip up the following concoctions. We all deserve a little mollycoddle, and you owe it to yourself to pamper your Life-Back-DOiT.

Indulging
Life-Back-DOiT

SPA DAY

Buy yourself a half dozen roses.

Hilarious Fact: If you put some Viagra in a vase, it will make your roses stand up straight for a week beyond when they would normally wilt. You have to admit, it creates a comical visual.

First, hold the six roses up to your face in the mirror and look at seven beautiful things!

Then get down to business toots … slip into some heavy yellow rubber gloves & scrub the tub. Heck, clean the whole bathroom and make it spa-like. Clean out all clutter and make it inviting. Or, go all out and rent a nice hotel room with a jacuzzi tub.

PRO TIP: It's much easier to drink wine in a bathtub than while taking a shower. I know.

DISCLAIMER (again): Consult with your physician and your best friend before using any of the Life-Back-DOITs in this book.

I've divided the process into a 3-day plan. It won't take three days, but you want to prepare everything the day before your debauchery, and implement a well-deserved indulgence the day after. You are worth it.

DAY 1

Gather your supplies and mix up your pampering potions before you start. Sometimes fancy spa products have ingredients you don't recognize. Neither will your body. But these products are familiar and easy to find. You probably have most of them.

Supplies:

- Your Favorite Wine Glass
- An extra wine glass for detox water
- Oatmeal
- Baking soda (sodium bicarbonate)
- Epsom Salt (magnesium sulfate)
- Sea Salt or Himalayan Salt
- Unfiltered and unprocessed Apple Cider Vinegar
- Olive Oil
- Coconut Oil
- Brown Sugar
- Honey
- Plain Yogurt
- Fresh Fruit (Lemons, Strawberries, bananas)
- Fresh Mint Leaves
- Cucumber
- Ground ginger
- Skin brush
- Cotton wipes or balls
- Shower cap
- Rubber gloves
- Heating pad
- Cozy warm blanket

- Scented candles
- Essential Oils – (not essential, but I suggest Rosemary and Lavender)
- Good Movies or Good Book
- Music
- Healthy snacks (like avocado, hummus, cheese, fruits & veggies)
- Bottle of Good Wine (or your favorite cocktail/mocktail)
- 2 Hand towels (or thick cotton socks) & a bowl to put 'em in

Read through the spa day tips before you begin and make everything ahead of time. You'll have plenty of product left over for an extra day or two of indulgence over the next few weeks.

Make Your Hot-Oil Hair Treatment

Pour 2 tbsp of olive oil into a bowl. Add a dollop of coconut oil and 2 tablespoons of honey. Heat it up in the microwave for 22 seconds (just before you use it). Mix. Rosemary essential oil promotes hair growth naturally, so add it to the mix if you've been pulling your hair out.

Make Water

THEY say you should drink half your body weight in ounces of water per day. If you weigh 200 lbs., drink 100 oz of water. Good luck with that. Water is boring, so to avoid the temptation to drink nothing but wine, mix up some Detox Water & let it sit in the fridge so that the water soaks up all the nutrients. Then drink it at room temperature. No ice. Below are two options for you:

Cucumber Water

Cucumber's diuretic properties help flush moisture from your body (bad moisture). Throw in a pinch of sea salt and some lemon slices for tart flavor and vitamins. Vitamins A & C help to reverse adverse effects of pollutants, abrasions, and other unwelcomed trauma … like divorce and mulch tragedy.

Sassy Water

Don't even wonder what it is, the name alone says you need it … you just add ginger to the water above. Ginger is one of the best herbs for losing weight, which can bring out your sassy.

Make More Water

Stop and smell the rose (water). Rose-water Toner Astringent is an expensive luxury, so make your own.

Take a rose from your bouquet & put it in a pretty vase in your bathroom. Then firmly pack one cup of rose petals & pour two cups of boiling water over the top. Cover and steep until cool. Strain and refrigerate in a sterilized jar.

Rosewater helps maintain the skin's pH balance, controls excess oil, and has anti-inflammatory/antibacterial/antioxidant properties. It also strengthens skin cells and regenerates skin tissues, tightens capillaries, and reduces eye puffiness and skin blotchiness. Who doesn't need Rose Water?

Make A Face Mask

For dry skin: Mix 1 teaspoon honey and 1 teaspoon olive oil

For regular skin: Mix 1 teaspoon honey and 1 mashed banana

(Here's where your extra potato-smasher comes in handy (again). Don't use the one dangling inspiring words.

For oily skin: Mix 1 teaspoon honey and 1 tablespoon oatmeal

Make a sugar scrub

1 cup brown sugar 1 cup raw oatmeal 1 cup olive oil

Get your Detox Bath Medley ready

Mix up ¼ cup (each) of oatmeal & mint leaves, Epsom Salt, and Baking Soda. Add 2 tablespoons (each) of Sea Salt & ground ginger. Stash it by the tub. Put aside ¼ cup of vinegar to add to your bath when you're ready to get in.

Set up the bathroom with candles (a lighter), and relaxing music. Prepare to slather the nourishing emollients on your body with love and attention. It's your only body, so appreciate it for what it is. Self-love and a sense of well-deserved extravagance are key to your spa day magic. Well, that and your beautiful wine glass.

DAY 2

Prepare a relaxation hideaway on the couch or in your bedroom with your snacks, beverages, another candle, and a book or movie.

With the mixology you prepared above, let the pampering begin. Dr. Phil said, "Time doesn't change us. It's what we do with that time that changes us." Take time to change your life for a day. (And don't feel bad about it! You're not being selfish.) Occasional self-indulgence doesn't mean "all about me," it means "me too."

Become a goddess for the day, and love the life you are living in this moment. Life isn't so much about finding yourself as it is about *creating* yourself. Create a luxurious morning or afternoon … just for you. If sad or frustrating thoughts creep into your mind, wash them away by focusing on the smell of your luxury and the tranquil atmosphere you have chosen for yourself today.

1. **Use Your Hot Oil Hair Treatment.**
    This soothing treatment is where the relaxation begins. It will also help moisturize and rejuvenate your hair, making it silkier and shinier. Apply the mixture to your hair and comb it through from

your roots. Tuck your hair into a shower cap, or wrap it in plastic wrap. Take a sip of your detox water.

2. **Time for the Best makeup remover ever.**
   Add a few drops of coconut oil to rosewater on a cotton pad to wipe off makeup and nourish your skin. Drink a little more water.

3. **Sugar scrub.**
   Exfoliate with the sugary scrub you've already prepared by massaging dry skin in slow circles, scrubbing gently all over (standing in the shower). Then rinse off. Your skin will feel like butter. Enjoy more detox water in a beautiful wine glass.

4. **Apply your Face mask & take a sip of water.**

5. **Turn on music; Light candles; Turn off the lights.**

6. **Draw a very warm bath.**
   It's nice if you have a little table beside the tub for your water. Drink more, but pee before you get in the tub. You know, hot water … relaxing … it happens.

Make your bath water deliciously moisturizing by adding your Detox Bath Medley.

Then pour in the vinegar and add lavender essential oils if you want to hype up the relaxation reflex. When the baking soda and vinegar mix, the water starts bubbling. Swish your bath concoction as you sing aloud, using your foot to swirl the water in the tub. Do it with a zestful spirit and optimism.

The minerals in a detox bath will help pull toxins from your skin, so drink another sip of your detox water before you submerge yourself in bliss (wine is waiting).

Start soaking and tranquilizing, allowing yourself at least 20 minutes in candlelight with soothing music. Focus on feeling peaceful. Breathe in the splendor you have reserved exclusively for yourself. Concentrate on every little luxury without thinking about anything else.

If unwelcomed thoughts creep into your garnished head, take a moment to sprawl in the benefits of your indulgence. Here are some feel-good details about what you're doing and what you're absorbing and expelling!

* Apple Cider Vinegar (full of vitamins, minerals, and enzymes) is one of the best ways to cleanse your body of bacteria and boost your immune system.
* Ginger sweats out toxins.
* Epsom Salt helps replenish your body's magnesium level, combating hypertension. Sulfate flushes toxins and helps form proteins in brain tissue and joints. I have no idea how it reaches your brain tissue, but THEY say it does.
* Baking soda cleanses with antifungal properties, leaving skin very soft.
* Sea Salt or Himalayan Salt - Composed of magnesium, potassium, calcium chloride, and bromides helps to replenish minerals critical to your skin's metabolism.
* Magnesium combats stress & fluid retention, slows skin aging and calms the nervous system.
* Calcium prevents water retention, increases circulation, and strengthens bones and nails.
* Potassium energizes the body and helps to balance skin moisture.
* Bromides relax your muscle stiffness.
* Sodium is important for lymphatic fluid balance (this in turn is important for immune system function).

7. **Now, relax again and be in the moment with your undeniable beauty. Give yourself a lymphatic massage.**
   The lymphatic system is a part of your body's defense system. Your lymph nodes are responsible for removing microorganisms and filtering bacteria from the bloodstream. With just five more minutes of bath lounging, you can stimulate your lymphatic system to detox your body—and appreciate your luxury.

8. **Place your fingers under your ears on either side of your neck.**

9. **With relaxed hands, gently pull your skin downward toward the back of your neck to the top of your shoulders on either side of your neck.**

10. **Gently massage your skin toward your shoulders and collarbones.**
    If you can find a single, seriously super-sexy next-door neighbor to do this for you, go for it.

11. **Relax for the remainder of your luxury soak, consciously releasing body tension.**
    Let go of worries, stress, and thoughts of kicking someone's ass.

Visualize the toxins exiting your body and the vitamins and nutrients entering their place. I imagine that Texas Trash Tramp soaking in my toxins & getting a pile of mulch dumped on HER head. Hey, laughter is therapeutic too! Wash it off.

12. **Drain the tub & rinse your face mask & hot oil treatment under the spigot, while you're still sitting.**
    Rinse your hair with rose water. Let it run down your body. Rose water adds shine, revitalizes hair growth, soothes mild scalp inflammations, and prevents dandruff. THEY say the aroma of roses is a powerful mood enhancer. It rids you of feelings of anxiety (especially after being buried in a pile of mulch).

13. **Get out of the tub (slowly).**
    You may get lightheaded and the tub is probably slippery, so don't lose that soothing feeling by falling on your ass.

14. **Splash some Rosewater on your face to tone and tighten.**
    (Rosewater can later be sprayed over makeup for a zingy glow.) You don't need makeup now, so bite the end of a vitamin E gel & put the Vitamin E all over your face. Top that with coconut oil.

Any time your body detoxes you need to replace fluids, so drink an additional wine glass full of detox water, then pour your favorite beverage into your beautiful crystal wine glass. If your favorite beverage is another glass of water, you're an admirable person. You're really into this! Otherwise, enjoy some great wine.

Wet two hand towels (if you don't have foot towels) or heavy cotton socks and microwave them for 52 seconds. Put them into a bowl & place it by your relaxation hideaway.

Rub olive oil and/or coconut oil on your feet, and wrap your feet in the towels or socks.

Consciously remember everything you are thankful for. Like today.

Generously slather olive oil or coconut oil (and frankincense if you want) on your hands & cuticles and slip-on rubber gloves. Yes, the ones you used to scrub the tub. For the softest hands ever, snuggle your gloved hands underneath a heating pad.

Curl up under a warm cuddly blanket with beverages & snacks and turn on a fun happy movie. Consider *The Holiday, Elf, My Fair Lady,* or *Nine to Five.* If you're not into watching movies, read a good book. Or, keep reading this one!

After a while, you may want to paint your nails or pluck some unwanted hairs from your face. Do whatever makes you feel like you are worthy of love and satisfaction: Because you are.

You're so hot—you can continue to detoxify through perspiration for another couple of hours. You're also hot because your body is now a magnificent glowing rag doll. Admit it; you're just hot, smokin' hot.

After a day like this, I know you'll be inspired to keep pampering yourself, and more inclined to take care of *You.* Keep going.

DAY 3

The morning after spa day, before your brain awakens to bombard your serenity, lie flat on your back and keep your lips together. Smile up into the sky, breathing deeply through your nose.

Stretch the length of your body, as if someone were pulling your heels off the end of the bed. Stretch your arms wide to the side. Push one heel toward the end of the bed and alternate, pushing from your hips to wake up your extremities and loosen your back.

Intertwine your fingers and stretch them, pushing your palms away from your face.

Lift your legs straight up; press your heels to the ceiling with toes toward your head; then point your toes toward the ceiling and flex your heels again until you wake them up.

Keep your legs in the air and spread them wide, letting gravity pull them apart; point and flex your feet, turning your knees outward and then forward … you're coming alive!

Bend your knees and grab your feet. Pull your toes back and feel the stretch in your feet.

Stand up with grace and dignity; make a big ball of "I'm marvelous in every way" by reaching your arms into the air, welcoming the new day. Look up into the universe. Take your hands to the floor and stretch your back, hips, and legs. I call this my version of "hello world I'm magnificent" (yoga fans call similar contortions sun salutation).

If you haven't already, go to the Jim. I call my bathroom the "Jim" instead of the "John." I like telling people I go to the Jim first thing every morning!

When you get to the Jim, if you happen to look in the mirror and see bags under your eyes, that's normal. Sometimes a good detox can slap you in the face with puffy eyes. The good news is: you can use bags to eliminate the bags.

Soak two tea bags in ice-cold water for 2 minutes. Caffeine constricts blood vessels to reduce swelling.

Squeeze the tea bags, lie down, close your eyes and gently press the tea bags over your eye bags for 9 minutes to displace excess fluid trapped around your eyes. Smile and be appreciative that you awakened today. Count 10 things that make you happy.

Now, look in the mirror and say to yourself – out loud:

- Damn girl, if you were a fruit, you'd be a FINEapple.
- Somebody call the cops because it must be illegal to look this good!

Just reading through spa day and imagining how good it feels is both relaxing and invigorating, but doing it is supremely better. So, DOiT!

DOiT Journal.

2 things you will accomplish today.

3 things that make you happy.

How did you feel after a luxury day for yourself? (Add those words to your Potato-Smasher.)

Potato-Smasher-Words:

Pamper, Wine, Indulgence, Almighty, Bliss, Virtuous, Healthy, Mollycoddle, Sweeter, Creative, Goddess, Vitalize, Soothe, Marvelous.

6

Didn't Need Those Pantyhose Afterall

"Humility will open more doors than arrogance ever will"
~Zig Ziglar

When a relationship dissolves, you feel like you lose control, and lose face. Or was that just me? A natural tendency is to recover a little respect by acting superior. Appearing indifferent to an embarrassing situation feels less humiliating. Like when you walk into a shut door, so you step back and slap it a few times like you're checking its sturdiness. Or, if you fall while dancing and immediately break out into "the worm," as if that's why you're on the floor. It's just a part of the dance!

We all try to rise above disgrace with as much subtle dignity as we can. It's not unusual to make a fool of yourself. Everyone does it. Just be sure you embarrass yourself without arrogance. That means you had better know how to laugh at yourself when you've done something moronic. You may as well join the crowd.

I was headed to my first funeral without a date. That was bad enough, but it was my brother's funeral, my only sibling. We were nothing alike, and he never liked me, but I spent our childhood taking up for my little brother. He wasn't perfectly likable either, but I loved him.

I drove into the city alone, with my truck covered in mud. Not wanting to fit in with the hillbilly side of the family, I decided to go through the automatic car wash before the funeral. Of course, this was one of the rare post-divorce occasions when I was in a nice dress, hose, and heels. I stopped for gas first. Being a multi-tasker, I also filled up the gas cans I haul around for the lawnmower, weed eater, and leaf blower.

I'm not sure if you know this, but climbing into the back of a truck bed to fetch gas cans, while wearing a little black dress, can cause a sophisticated woman to lose a shoe under the truck and rip her hose. Retrieving my shoe wasn't a dignified endeavor. Let's just leave it at that.

Nearby gas patrons didn't even offer to assist me. Whatever happened to chivalry? I do understand though; when I laugh uncontrollably, I am also too weak to move or assist an idiot. How's that for not being a redneck hillbilly?

With 16 minutes to spare, I raced to the most exclusive drive-through car wash in the city ... the one with the long, exquisite floppy flappers. I was sitting peacefully behind the wheel, listening to classical music, thinking how appropriate it was that I had such an eloquent option. It was uncanny that I had to drive 68 miles to have a robot wash my truck in 9 minutes when it takes me 88 minutes to wash it with a ladder and a hose back at the cabin. It sure would be nice if I lived close enough to walk to a car wash!

I decided to simply indulge in the experience. It was like being at a truck spa—so relaxing, effortless, and satisfying. I deserved this luxury. I was a refined, professional, divorced woman.

As the colorful suds began their delicate dance and moved toward the truck, I realized I hadn't folded my mirrors back. Since I wanted to keep them attached to the truck, I lowered the automatic windows and reached out to fold the mirror back—just as the first rubber slapper met my window area ... and my face.

I was still locked into my seatbelt as the frothy, billowing pink and green suds coated my body and the interior of my truck. I had accidentally lowered all four windows. I knew I couldn't close any of them for fear of trapping the unnecessarily huge rubber assailants. Who knows; that sadistic parasite may have slammed my truck back into the car behind me if my windows captured its bombarding appendages.

I never got to the mirror on the passenger side to push it back. But the moving mechanical zombie machine attacking my truck took care of that for me. I replaced the mirror shortly thereafter.

If you've never experienced a face-to-face encounter with those fluorescent flappers, or don't realize how heavy and intrusive they can be, let me tell you. They reach into the middle of a truck and wrap around a driver's head, neck, and upper torso. It's like being attacked by a giant sea squid.

I slapped back and thrashed around to battle them the best I could as the tentacles assaulted me from every angle, from every window. I looked around for the cameras. I was seemingly debuting in a "Three Stooges" episode, all by myself. The left side of my face was slapped as I flopped to the right—for yet another slap from the other side. The foam washing over me was like a pie in the face.

Finally, the invasion moved from the back seat to the bed of my truck, and I raised the windows. But that was kind of stupid, because I missed the rinse cycle, and had to use my entire stash of fast-food napkins to wipe suds from my hair and dignified attire.

Why didn't I think to open the windows again when the high-powered blowers dried the exterior of my truck?

Running late (as usual), I had no time to clean up, so to speak. So, I ended up going to the funeral with a shiny clean truck, wet hair, and makeup that looked like I'd cried all night in a drunken stupor. At least I wasn't naked, this time. My coffee was knocked off the holder between the seats, but since it was my lucky day, none spilled on my dress, and coffee made my feet smell, well, better.

My dad and cousins were standing outside the church door when I screeched into a parking space. I regained my dignity, gathered my pride, then jumped to get out of my truck with the seat belt buckled. They looked at me like I had a dead cat on my head.

My cousin said, "I'm not even going to ask." So, I didn't tell.

I wondered if anyone noticed after the funeral that the potato salad and pot pie tasted a little like soap suds?

I couldn't help but think I should just stay in the country now. I realized that I'd become a hick, as I sat unashamedly with my kindred at the funeral. They never expected me to be dignified anyway.

Some professed, at the graveyard, that they were dang impressed by my side-mirror duct-taping skills. I felt proud and consequently less arrogant. I reckoned that I couldn't feel too big for my britches anymore.

Acceptance from my hillbilly kin-folk made it plain to me that a little taste of rigmarole, doused with some humility is easier to swallow than an overly-spiced high-falootin' opinion of oneself. The possum-pot-pie, however, was a different story.

Never underestimate the power of humility. It often exposes a cleansing, face-slappin' revelation, and puts us in our place. No matter how polished we think we are, we simply are what we are. What a relief to finally feel like I belong where I am.

Should you ever come to the Blue Ridge Mountains of Virginia, you may want to brush up on gettin' along with people around here. Learning the customs and lingo, becoming familiar with the folks at the local flea market, and learning to play the banjo will help. I'll share some Appalachian Hillbilly recognition and survival skills to help you fit in.

If you get a hankerin' to live a simpler life in the hills, you gotta learn a few lessons from the following guide I assembled for you. You'll never regret it - if you DOiT.

You are welcome.

Y'alls
Life-Back-DOiT

First of all, there's nothing wrong with a muddy truck. Mud reveals that you're using a truck properly.

Next, you need to know your redneck n' yer hillbilly. There's a difference. The term "redneck" comes from the fact that farmers get sunburnt on the backs of their necks from being outside all day. Thus, a redneck is sometimes a farmer or vice versa. Rednecks are also identified as those who are uncouth and uncultured because they grew up in working-class families, far from the influence of urban culture.

Rednecks evolved in the late 1800s in southern West Virginia when the coal miners fought the owners of the mines. My granddaddy survived the Matewan Massacre as a Baldwin Felts detective back then. The rebelling miners wore red bandanas around their necks, and Granddaddy said that's why they were called "rednecks."

Rednecks are sometimes associated with guns and a kind of prideful ignorance. Rednecks don't necessarily live in the hills, but a "hillbilly" *is* someone who lives in the hills—commonly the Appalachian Mountains. Sometimes William from Kentucky was called "a Billy from the Hills." A hillbilly plays bluegrass music sittin' on the couch on their front porch. Hillbillies judge no one and may have fewer teeth than rednecks. There is a sense of innocence in hillbilly living.

Lots of Hillbillies were coal miners. Coal country was a melting pot of Irish, Scottish, black, white, Chinese, Italian, English, Greek, and German. That's how bluegrass music came about. African Americans from the southernmost states brought the banjo to the Appalachians and mixed sound with mandolins, guitars, and front porch mountain music (spoons, washboards, etc.). Fiddles from Ireland chimed in to create a beautiful sound.

If it weren't for the coal, we wouldn't have bluegrass. If it weren't for bluegrass, we wouldn't have flat footin.' Flat footin' is how we dance to bluegrass music, and it takes stamina, and a lack of pride, to shuffle your feet furiously with your arms dangling by your sides.

Both rednecks and hillbillies have their own philosophy of living. They wash their own truck in their own front yard without any fancy machinery. Both work daylight to dark every day, pay their own way, "don't ask the government for nothin' and don't want the government in their beeswax."

Country folk, whether redneck or hillbilly, are generally good-hearted, good-mannered, hard-workin' simple folk who respect their elders and show lots of pride in the flag and the casseroles they take to church picnics and funerals.

The following are quotes from bona fide hillbillies and rednecks...

"I do know that we rednecks have amazing survival skills; we're the only ones left to talk to news crews after a natural disaster, and I know I can call my neighbors if I need help. They'll grab the duct tape and a rag to cover the wound then haul my ass to the nearest vet for emergency stitches."

A "redneck" can mean a snitch, too. Hillbillies say: ``You redneck on somebody, you just straight-out told the law what people was doin.'' Redneckin' gets you beat the f*** up.

"You ain't from 'round here, are ya?" (We all say that.)

"I grew up in a holler. My grandpa used to make moonshine up in that holler. A holler's where you can step out on yer front porch and go, 'Hey, you got any 'maters?' and they'll holler back, 'Yeah! You got any rhubarb?'"

HOW TO IDENTIFY A REDNECK:

More than one of their living relatives is named after a Southern Civil War general.

They think the last words to The Star-Spangled Banner are "Gentlemen, start your engines."

They spent more on their pickup truck than on their education.

Taking a dip has nothing to do with water.

They have a rag for a gas cap.

The hood and one door are a different color from the rest of their truck, and the mirror on the side is attached with duct tape. (Just so you know, I only used duct tape a few weeks before I had a body shop attach mine in the standard manner.)

They believe "He needed killin'" is a valid defense.

WHAT REDNECKS SAY:

"It's colder than a witch's tit in a brass bra in January."

"Lick" (verb), as in, "I licked him good that time" (that means he got the F beat up).

"Lick" (noun) - any amount, such as, "I didn't get a lick o' work done today because that case o' beer took the getty-up outta my go."

"Yapper " – mouth (most likely he didn't get a lick of work done because he never stops runnin' his yapper either).

"Useless as tits on a bull" - utterly useless.

"He's about as handy as a back pocket on a shirt."

HOW TO IDENTIFY A HILLBILLY:

They think possum is "The Other White Meat."

They have flowers planted in a bathroom appliance in the front yard.

When you ask for directions, you should know that "Just down the road a piece" can be 1 mile or 7. It's just over yonder past where Billy Ray's deer stand used to be.

They call a potato: a "tater," and an animal: a "varmint."

Hillbilly 10-year-olds have their own shotguns; they are proficient marksmen, and mamma taught 'em how to aim (always above the breast of a turkey).

WHAT HILLBILLIES SAY:

"Shoot, lemme think."

"Well slap yer granny."

"He can't carry a tune in a bucket."

"Gussied up" - cleaned up and dressed very nicely.

"Reckon" – as in, "I reckon we'll see you at the reunion." (He'll probably get gussied up for that.)

"I got a hankerin' fer…".

"You need that like you need a hole in the head!" Obviously, you do not need a hole in your head; it's even bad for you. Thus, anything you definitely don't need is described this way.

"Skedaddle" - to leave hurriedly.

"Well that just dills my pickle."

"Well, don't you look purtier than a glob o' butter meltin' on a stack of wheat cakes!"

"He's so dumb he could throw himself on the ground n' miss."

"Ain't no point in beatin' a dead horse, 'Course, can't hurt none neither."

"Excuses are like backsides; Everybody's got one and they all stink."

Rednecks and hillbillies sometimes go off and if they do, there's a difference between a hissy fit and a conniption fit, and you don't "have" them, you "pitch" 'em. I guess that goes without sayin.'

If you're having a hard time understanding all this hillbilly redneck stuff, bless your heart. Get some sweet tea or fill up your wine glass and keep tryin.' Just don't think you can claim to be a redneck or a hillbilly by simply learnin' the lingo and sporting your overalls tucked into your workin' boots. After all, if a cat had kittens in the oven, we wouldn't call 'em biscuits.

Love your family and embrace every opportunity you have to be with them. When they are gone, you may wish you'd said something to make amends or to let them know how much you appreciate them. You can reap a lot o' learnin' from yer kinfolk.

DOiT Journal.

Name one thang that ain't necessarily proper, but you're proud to Do
Name one thang that ain't necessarily proper, but you're proud to Know
Name one thang that ain't necessarily proper, but you're proud to Have
Make a list of fond memories to share with family members.

Ask questions about the lives of people you're kin to. Get to know them better and write down their stories to share with future generations.

Draw a family tree. Below each name—put a complimentary word that describes them.

Plan a family reunion and share your family tree.

Potato-Smasher-Words:

Exquisite, Eloquent, Respect, Pride, Dignity, Peaceful, Stultifying, Good-Hearted, Bliss.

7

Face Fear with the Appropriate Weapon

"Courage isn't a lack of fear. It's being terrified by what you face, yet doing what has to be done. That's a dose of humility."
~Debbie Craig

It takes courage to face life on your own. Especially if you are taking care of other humans. Think about it though: how many challenges would you face if you were not forced to do so? Well, maybe the ice bucket challenge, for a worthy cause. But who wouldn't take the elevator instead of the stairs at the Empire State Building?

We usually take the easy way out; it's a no-brainer. Not having a choice, though, will lead you to brave accomplishments and a sense of triumph. Courage can be simultaneously intoxicating and hair-raising.

You can't always make fear disappear, but you can face it and challenge it. Something good will come from everything bad that happens to you—if you learn to turn it around (even if it's just in your head). That sounds idealistic, but I've lived long enough to know it's true. Bad things happen, and when they do, don't wallow in it. Take control of hairy situations and you can guide the outcome or, at least, run fast enough to escape with graceful splendor.

Months after I ceased being intimidated by the cabin "settling" and trees swaying in the wind, I was on the computer when I heard faint noises downstairs. I was proud of the fact that it was dark outside and I hadn't locked myself into the safety of my bedroom, yet.

Empowered by the confidence that a good Merlot instills, I was hardly frightened when an unexplainable commotion broke out behind the downstairs door. Okay, admittedly my heart jumped, and I almost passed out, but I sat stoic and unrattled with my fingers firmly committed to a Facebook post.

I had learned to ignore most noises around the cabin unless they caused a fire or a bathroom emergency. But when I heard the clunking up and down my stairs a third time, I put the wine glass down and calmly ran to the bedroom for my pistol.

My son taught me to shoot. I am a crack shot. I nearly shot a squirrel once … relatively speaking. There was a squirrel in a tree, and I shot in the general direction of the tree with a squirrel on the limb.

OK, I was a little uneasy, but it's not like I was scared to death. Granted, I did think I might die when I became acutely aware of the symptoms I'd suddenly developed. I was sick to my stomach; pretty sure I was about to have one of those bathroom emergencies and felt like I'd contracted a severe nervous disorder. As the intrusion became more obvious, I was so wobbly I could hardly pick up those tiny bullets.

In a state of mild hysteria, I was faced with memory loss. How the heck was I supposed to open up that circular part of the gun to put ammunition into the holes? I should have brought my beautiful wine glass with me when I locked myself in the bedroom. If these were my last moments, I should have my wine glass! But there was no way I was going to face the intruder single-handedly without the advantage of a loaded gun.

Eventually, I discovered the little lever that made the cylinder pop out. I pushed the bullets in – nipples pointing toward the shaft (hey, it's better than no sex at all). I grabbed my car alarm and cell phone (with 911 ready to send when things got out of control). Then I went back to the kitchen for a quick swig of courage from my favorite wine glass before proceeding.

Standing at the top of the stairs (still behind the closed door), I took a respectable 11 minutes to make sure I wasn't imagining the noise. Nope; I clearly heard someone downstairs squirreling around, probably wrangling the TV and all my best wine. My wine! That hastened my courage.

Mustering my moxie, I threw the door wide and called to the crowd of nonexistent men guarding me. I wanted whoever was down there to believe I wasn't alone, so I yelled, "cover my back; I'm going down; the police are on their way ... no I will go, just don't point your shotguns toward me."

That created even more commotion downstairs.

After painfully creeping (with my back against the wall) down creaky stairs, I strategically jumped around the corner to flush out the housebreaker. The silent room was empty, and I realized he was back behind the bar, in the laundry room, or in the bathroom. The French doors were locked from the inside. They usually are, but that was creepy.

Just around the next corner, I was faced with a decision. Should I start shooting toward the ceiling, sneak up on him (them?), or jolt into the bathroom with a confident yelp?

I called to my imaginary backup team: "don't come down, you go around, I'll stand my ground!" Rolling my eyes ... why did I rhyme *now*? That sounded poetically weak ... as were my knees.

I stormed the bathroom, popping around the corner with more of a scream than a yelp. He wasn't there. I swung around to face him, but thankfully, he wasn't there either. Nor was he behind the bar, or in the laundry room.

He couldn't have gotten back up the stairs. His boots were so big I would have heard him. I fervently checked every hiding place until I came upon my multi-tiered plant stand in the front corner of the room.

I screamed when I spotted him, and he had no reaction—as if I were not a threat. He just sat there, staring back at me, with absolutely no fear of my pointed gun and cell phone!

Right there in my Aloe Vera plant was a little baby varmint of some sort. It looked like a baby bat. But I couldn't make myself get close enough to identify him.

I hadn't called my son this time because I wasn't sure if it was another false alarm. The fourth time I called him to save me from cabin noises, he just said "Ok mama, let me know what happens." He was the son who drove an hour to confront the shadow lurking outside my window (the flag). My kids love me.

Feeling fearless because I hadn't pushed 911 to report a baby squirrel in my plants, I ran outside and grabbed my long-reach pond skimmer, picking up my wine glass on the way back though. I descended the stairs and proceeded to chase Rocky around the room. (Of course I named him.) Then I knocked over a lamp with the end of the long pond-net handle.

Opening both sets of doors, I finally coaxed him outside. Then he scurried around and re-entered through the other doors. It reminded me of that Ray Stevens song about the day a squirrel went berserk in church "...a fight for survival that broke out in revival...".

I chased Rocky outside again, slamming the door behind him, and slipped on the rug, falling into the bookshelf (where my wine glass sat). I almost shot myself (accidentally of course). He ran inside the other door once more and settled back into my plants, where he fell asleep—with his little furry friend! Two of them. I hadn't seen Bullwinkle. He was a sleeper.

I wasn't going to pick them up, and obviously, I couldn't corral them, so I shot them (with my camera). I shared their photos on social media, and they appreciated the exposure but had no intentions of going anywhere.

My motherly instinct was to let them sleep, but my tenured position as head of the nut-house led me to awaken them and finally shoo them out the door into the cold spring night. I almost felt guilty. They had been cuddled together in a cute little cozy ball. They were just babies.

But I can't be everyone's mother. Did you know that squirrels can't burp? It doesn't matter; they had to go. I just hope being kicked out of the cabin didn't depress them. There's nothing worse than a depressed squirrel.

Richard Cranium used to hunt squirrels, back when we were in High School. Country folk and frontiersmen eat squirrels. I've tried to cook them before, but they were always terribly tough and rubbery. So, I pulled out my grandmother's old cookbook and remembered just how tender baby squirrels vacationing in a planter could have tasted. Motherly instincts dismissed.

Walt Disney said something like "the whole thing was started by a mouse." (A rodent—with a big bushy tail, in my case.) If you are bestowed the unsolicited gift of squirrels to cook, don't act like a nut; just trust the following recipe. I promise it's better than my failed attempts to disguise bushy-tailed mouse meat as tenderloin to impress RC.

Walt Disney also said, "If you can dream it, you can…" DOiT.

A Squirrely
Life-Back-DOiT

Squirrels have been proven to run at speeds of 20 miles per hour and can see behind them; that explains a lot. So instead of running around the house to catch your squirrel, engage a hillbilly to hunt some down (when in season, of course). You must admit, when grocery stores feel empty, those pesky squirrels (who relentlessly empty your bird feeders) look tastier and tastier. Turn the tables by turning them into supper.

Skippy Squirrel Stew

(Compliments of Grandmaw's recipe and Chef Loren's revisions.)

1. Skin 4 squirrels (If you only have 2, supplement with skinned chicken or pork loin).
2. Soak squirrels in saltwater overnight. This helps get rid of gamey flavor and makes the meat tender. Remove, rinse, and drain.
3. Rub the squirrel with tenderizer. (Make sure he's dead first.)
4. Add squirrel to a cast-iron skillet and cook on high until browned on all sides.
5. Place squirrel in a crockpot.
6. Cover with lightly-salted water and cook on high for 2-3 hours or until meat starts to fall off the bone.
7. Remove the squirrel and allow it to cool.
8. Save the broth if you want gravy.
9. Remove meat from the bones and cut it into cubes.

If you haven't acquired squirrel meat, skip the steps above and just use chicken or pork:

Ingredients:

- 4 cups cubed meat
- 1 can tomato sauce
- 1 cup chicken stock
- 1 Tbsp fresh cracked black pepper
- 1 Tsp white pepper
- 2 Tsp blackened seasoning
- 1/2 cup red wine
- 2 Tbsp olive oil
- 2 Tbsp kosher salt
- 1 Tbsp thyme

- 1 Tbsp oregano
- 1/4 cup chopped parsley
- 3 cloves minced garlic
- ½ yellow onion sliced thin
  (Avoid cutting yourself when slicing onion by having someone else hold it while you chop.)

1. Bring the olive oil to high heat in the large cast-iron skillet. Wait for a hint of smoke.
2. Add cubed meat and brown on all sides, stirring infrequently to build a good fond and sear on the pan.
3. Deglaze the pan with chicken stock and/or red wine (I asked Chef Loren, and that's just gourmet talk for "lift the fond off the pan by deglazing into the stew." (I'm still not sure; I think it means stir liquid into the pan to create gravy.)
4. Add tomato sauce and all the other ingredients, reserving half of the parsley.
5. Cook at medium heat for about 25 minutes until the meat is tender.
6. Serve over your favorite pasta, rice, or a fresh batch of buttermilk biscuits.

You need more than two hours to get two squirrels out of your house. The same thing goes when cooking a squirrel. They need lots of time to tenderize; otherwise, they taste like deer jerky.

(As a Bona Fide Hillbilly, I know these things.)

Enjoy. Enjoy even more by serving your guests without telling them what they're eating!

It's crazy how your mind distorts reality when you encounter an unfamiliar ingredient—or an unfamiliar varmint. Don't jump to conclusions, but imagine the best scenario for your concern. Find inspirational stories about things that scare you. You're probably not the only person with those apprehensions. You're definitely not the only person who has been deserted or wronged. Acknowledge your fears, face them, and don't back down. It could just be fear of the unknown.

BTW: Hippopotomonstrosesquippedaliophobia (ironically) is the fear of long words. I hope that didn't frighten you.

> ## DOiT Journal.
>
> Name three fears you don't want to face.
>
> (Perhaps public speaking, relatives, or being stalked by a possum.)
>
> What weapon will you use to battle those fears? (Maybe humor, a change of scenery, a reality check?)
>
> Document something you've done that made you feel brave.

Potato-Smasher-Words:

Courage, Intoxicating, Moxie, Empowered, Graceful, Sex, Cozy, Vacationing, Trust, Try, Gravy, Inspirational, Tender.

8

Friends in Low Places

"Humility is not thinking less of yourself; it's thinking of yourself less."
~C.S. Lewis

Do you feel like you're the only person to suffer from being crushed and shattered? If you tune in to someone else's playlist, you will hear a different chorus. You (probably) don't own the rights to the world's saddest love song. Countless musicians and poets have experienced excruciating romantic disappointments long before you were even born. Artistic people confess that sad situations make them feel more acutely alive and throw them into creative mode.

Appreciate the fact that misery loves company, and you're not alone. When you've been left to rebuild a life on your own, you're not the only one. That's proof that you too will survive. When you're struggling to make sense of it all, this transition in your life can be the defining event that forces you to redefine yourself in a positive, resourceful way.

Take a peek at what other women have done when faced with adversity. I'd like to introduce you to some women who pulled themselves through infidelity, humiliation, and divorce. They were good at retaliation. Everyone has a story. And, ok, I also shared another of mine, I had to, for contrast.

Sweet Caroline

My beautiful friend, Caroline, was married to a wealthy investor. He was a pilot, a bodybuilder, and the father of her son. He was a typical devoted family man. They had dinner parties, pool parties, and family nights during their 25 years of marriage. They had an impressive group of aristocratic friends and were both very active in the community and in their church.

It turns out that Caroline's husband was much more active in the church than she realized: He was pumping their church's young organist. Somehow that conjures up too many visuals about organs. Anyway, Caroline was devastated when she found out. During her agonizing, sleepless nights at home alone, she posted descriptive and truthful comments on social media about the what-who-with of the church's organist and her husband.

Once it was publicly obvious what was going on, some of her church family asked to visit Caroline at her home. She was comforted by the thought of their support, knowing they would help her through the devastation of discovering that her husband was playing with the organist. She cherished these friends, who had been at their wedding and the baptism of their son, and Caroline was looking forward to the guidance and comfort they would bring.

That's not what they brought. Instead, they requested that she not post anything about any parishioners on social media anymore. You know, for the *dignity* of the members.

Caroline had been sharing more than her dinner menu with her "Friends" and followers, and the congregation was embarrassed by her testimony. After their fellowship, Caroline was overwhelmingly compelled to agree that she shouldn't shame or expose her very prominent husband and the church organist on the internet, to maintain the respectability of the parish.

Caroline was principled and dedicated to her word, so she stifled her burning desire to share the scandal with the cyberworld. The following Sunday, she went to church as usual. Being the dignified socialite she had always been, Caroline graciously greeted her friends and acquaintances at the church door, offering each one a thoughtfully prepared flier with photos of her husband and the organist, detailing their affair.

The flier tastefully highlighted the score of their composition, and several other descriptive words referring to organ music. It was the least she could do to show her appreciation for the support from that hypocritical little town in Massachusetts. You gotta love her. She kept her word and didn't discuss her cheating husband with anyone at church or on social media again. They had her hand-out.

If anyone had missed church that Sunday, they likely saw the flier on community bulletin boards and store windows throughout the town. Caroline moved to Tennessee.

Oh Mandy

Another girlfriend, Mandy, was married for about a year. She wanted to surprise her husband with a romantic dinner, so she left work two hours early to pick up steaks and get ready before he came home.

Mandy unloaded groceries and lit the grill. Her husband, and her good friend, didn't even hear her enter the bedroom. She said they were "going at it" and didn't see her standing there with her .38 Special, at first.

They both stopped what they were doing and finally paid attention to Mandy when they heard her cock her gun. She told her friend, "Get the hell out." Her "friend" said, "let me get dressed first."

Mandy said, "you can get dressed and get shot, or leave immediately and take your chances." The "friend" ran out the door and Mandy fired a "warning" shot into the air. (That's how we hillbillies do it when we're looking to make a point.)

Mandy's husband came running out and tried to take the gun from her, but you know how insult, passion, and fury all wrapped around infidelity gives you strength? Well, Mandy found that strength and shot the gun over her young husband's head, emptying the .38 as he ran around the yard naked.

She said the best part of it was hearing her friend's screams as she ran naked down the street while watching her husband's limp dick pee down his leg.

Mandy went to her parents' house in time to overhear the phone conversation between her father and her husband. Her husband had called a State Trooper. Mandy's dad (the State Trooper) said, "well if Mandy had intended to shoot you, you wouldn't be talking to me right now."

Count on Your Friends

This is one of my exploits that demonstrates the importance of having a friend. Friends, usually, don't abandon you when you need them the most. Usually.

RC was sleeping with an Officers' Club bartender. During this time, he didn't show up for work repeatedly (in the Marine Corps)! I saved him from court-martial because I was friends with the Commanding Officer and his wife. (That story is for another book, so I'll cut to the chase, so to speak.)

RC had encouraged me to move our three sons to Virginia for better schools until he could get a transfer. But the transfer didn't come. Shortened version: RC and the bar slut totaled my BMW on New Year's Eve. They left the car (titled in my name) on the side of the road, so the police called my mom to report the "accident." I can only imagine what made him crash. She may have laid her head on his lap because she was tired.

RC and the bar slut were banging in the new year in New Orleans as I drove six hours to my friend, Lil's, house in Texas from my failed attempt to surprise him for the new year. I couldn't find him. I somehow thought he would be happy to see me. You know, since we were married and all.

After mom called early in the morning on January 1st to tell me about the police report on my vehicle and to make sure I was still alive, I called around base to get the story. Lil sat beside me and cried as I became increasingly calm learning the details of RC's shenanigans. Fury makes me suddenly cool-headed sometimes. Lil and I drove back to New Orleans, straight to the Officer's Club bar (where the whore bartended).

We sat down at the bar and asked who Dennie was (I knew the floozie's name). The men around the bar pointed to a slimy skinny skank mixing a drink. I couldn't stop laughing! I pulled out my Canon and started shooting pictures. The camera flashes attracted her attention and she slinked over to me and asked why I wanted her photo.

I said, "you make me so happy! I'm RC's wife and I can't wait to show his mother and sisters the scum he has been sleeping with! I am so relieved; I thought you would be so much more! They are going to love this; no one will believe it. We never expected it to be someone so sleazy." I just couldn't stop talking.

I hadn't planned what I would do when I found her. I had no idea what would happen when I got there, but everything just came naturally. It was an infamous night in my journey to divorce. I told Lil, "I have never punched anyone ever" (maybe my brother once, in self-defense). But I was overwhelmingly inclined to punch the barmaid in her face!

I don't like violence, and hurting someone is nothing I've ever wanted to do. But for some reason, that evening, all I wanted from life was to punch the bar slut in the face! She had an arrogance that manifested her power of being the hot attraction for lonely drunken men sitting around a bar. She made some snide remarks that I've erased from memory. I just remember that her comments seriously fueled my need to knock her out.

Of all people, my most dramatic friend kept telling me not to hit her. But I couldn't process her logic. I just knew that if I were ever to have the gumption to punch someone someday, this was my best opportunity! I was justified and I was all pumped up. I still can't believe I didn't do it. I so wanted to. I know, I was disappointed too.

The following night, Lil and I went to Dennie's apartment. Lil was driving. RC's car was parked in Dennie's space. Well, here's where it gets dicey. I finally got my revenge. I jumped out of Lil's car and sauntered over to the bar slut's shiny new Jeep, stalking it. I still had no plan. So, I decided to pee on her tire.

Yes, I did. Ok, that had about as much impact as getting hit by a parked car. But I was bad. I felt bad-ass.

As I shamelessly marked the bartender's tires, Lil slowly drifted her car away from the Jeep. I stumbled after my transportation in a panic, with my shorts around my ankles, and threw myself into the passenger seat. As I scrambled to pull up my pants, I demanded, "why would you leave me at a time like this!"

Lil looked at me in disgust as she sped away. She screamed at me: "Peeing on her tire? Really? That's all you've got? They were on the other side of her jeep, about to get in."

RC was gallantly opening the passenger door for her. How sweet.

I hadn't seen them, and that was probably a good thing because who knows what I would have done next. I'd surely have shown my ass in more ways than one if I had seen them together. You know I would. Something would have happened. I just hope he recognized my backside.

It probably took me longer to get over that infidelity because I never acquired the satisfaction of getting even. Yeah, yeah, I am pathetic about getting revenge. But I still have my dignity.

Don't I?

When you feel hurt and insecure, it's just so hard to be creative. Indubitably, I have no good ideas for revenge. But my friends do!

Oh Beth, the Things You Do

My girlfriend, Beth, started socializing immediately after her divorce. She trolled the bars and attended parties with another single girlfriend, Pam. Beth fell in love with Larry, and they became engaged. Just like a Hallmark movie.

Well, maybe not so much. Sadly, Beth learned that Larry was sleeping with her friend, Pam. Beth was a bad chooser of both men and girlfriends.

Beth said nothing to either of them, but she invited Pam to attend a big party with her in West Virginia, more than two hours away. They drove back into the country roads of WV for a few hours until Beth stopped at a remote gas station and gave Pam $5 to go inside for a pack of cigarettes they were going to share.

When Pam went inside the store, Beth backed out of the parking lot and drove home. She never spoke another word to either Larry or Pam for the rest of her life. Leaving Pam stranded in the mountains on a Saturday night was so much more impressive than peeing on a stupid tire. My friends are amazing!

My oldest and dearest friends and I have realized over the years that the reason we still trust each other is that we've never had a reason to ditch the other in the West Virginia mountains.

My true friends and I have unspoken codes of friendship:

- If you like him, and so do I, I will not look at him again, and I will become completely undesirable to him. No matter how much work it takes.
- If you like him, and I despise him, I will tell you why, in great detail, until you get rid of him (it took me 30+ years to listen to my friends about RC). I'm a slow learner.
- If you're exposing a booger or have a hair growing out of your chin, hell yes, a real friend will tell you about it.

Friends are like boobs; it doesn't take long to discover if they're real or fake. You know your girlfriend will call you in the morning, no matter what you did the night before. Don't lose touch, because you need friends; plan a girlz get-together and get your Life Back - DOiT.

Girls Just Wanna Have Fun and get their
Life-Back-DOiT

When RC and I worked and lived in the Middle East, there was nothing to do but entertain ourselves. We got creative. The Marine Security Guards, Ambassador, and embassy personnel are much more fun out of the country than they are in DC, and I have videos to prove it! (Call me for censorship fees. Just kidding.)

Use some of the following tried and terrific escapades to create your girlfriend gathering!

* **Game Night**: We put together a Wheel-of-Fortune night. One of our gay guy friends dressed fabulously as Vanna White to spin our homemade cardboard wheel. We made up questions about people and happenings in the embassy and places around the country. It was hilarious! Vanna stole the show.
If you want to make gaming a monthly event, start a Bunco group.
Everyone gets a chance to host once a year. The game is mindless enough to engage in conversation (aka gossip) while you play, and it's fun to take home some extra cash or a prize.

* **Video Lip-Sync Party**: Direct and film your independent entertainment. Think about it; how many songs can you lip-sync and act out? Invite everyone to plan a song, bring props and costumes, and take turns performing for the camera. After a day of hanging out with friends, you can spend the evening watching your production together. Or do it by yourself

and YouTube/TikTok your talent. You might even be discovered (hopefully not by your parents or children).

* **Wine Tasting:** Bring your favorite wine glass and present the wine you bring, elegantly describing the bouquet and comparing the color to something silly. Tell your own story about how and where it is made. Don't forget to describe the winemaker and his "grapes." Discuss the sweet full body, and don't forget the legs when describing the complexity of your unique vintage to your girlfriends. Design a personalized label to cover the original one.

* **Pool Party:** (Especially if you don't have a pool.) Just have everyone bring an hors d'oeuvre and turn on the sprinkler. We once purchased a large kiddie pool and five of us splashed around all day like dorky dolphins. Water ballet is always advisable. A sprinkler, pool, or puddle is playfully perfect for a hot day, especially if it's the same day as your Wine Tasting! Hire a pool boy to stop by to mix you another drink and hand you a towel.

* **Tap into your Talents**: Take a tap dance class, play the drums, learn pottery, or attend a paint and wine night together.

* **Sleep-Over Spa Night**: Assign each person one of the homemade spa treatments from chapter 5 and pamper yourselves together. Everyone must tell the story of their first kiss, their first time, or their last time. Take group photos in your face masks, watch movies and fall asleep in your sheet tents or under the stars in sleeping bags.

* **Wardrobe Wipeout Night:** Everyone goes through their closets and brings 16 items they haven't worn for 16 months. Display your unwanted merchandise on a rope tied across the room and on the dining table. Take turns picking out one thing. Once you have your stash, take turns modeling. Strut your stuff, runways style. If you like it, and the girls agree it's "you," you keep it. Shoes, purses, hats, gloves, dresses, tops, bottoms, skirts, swimsuits … anything you want to trade.

* **Not a Bachelorette Party:** You'll need penis paraphernalia, magic markers, T-shirts, and a fake veil. Go to an area with more than one bar,

and take turns being the bride-to-be at each bar. Dance like it's your last night of freedom. Have your shirts signed, and enjoy complimentary beverages and frivolous non-committal attention. Tell stories that will entertain the entire establishment and take plenty of photos! It will be just as much fun for people you've never met as it will be for you and your friends. Uber, Lyft, or designate a driver.

* **Dress Mismatched, Including Shoes.** Go to a department store, pull lawn chairs over to the demo TV area, and ask a salesperson to order pizza for you.

DOiT Journal.

Name your friends who would never give you a reason to abandon them in the mountains of West Virginia

Do you have unspoken Friendship codes?

What are they?

How does it make you feel to be liked?

Who would you like to become friends with? (You know, if it were anyone at all)?

Why?

Potato-Smasher-Words:

Goodness, Guidance, Comfort, Rejoice, Friendship, Fun, Frivolous, Freedom, Active, Support, Principled, Dedicated, Amazing, Impressive, Humorous, Silly, Unique.

9

This Mama Don't Sleep in the Outhouse

"Life is a long lesson in humility."
~Sir James Matthew Barrie

Everything you do changes something around you. THEY say that for every action there is an equal and opposite reaction. Hopefully, it's for the better, like when you burn the bread at every meal and your family learns to enjoy the unique culinary char. Or you get beastly sick and lose 8 pounds. See how something good comes from just-about everything?

Have you noticed that when you do nothing, nothing much develops? But when you act, something happens. Life changes, you change, and something changes every day. You don't have to change to make things better, but doing things better will change things for you. Everything and everyone you interact with is altered, just like fire transforms everything it touches.

My boys called me mommy. That changed. When they were teenagers, they called me mom. But for some reason, after the divorce, they called me mama. I think they thought it was funny and I just thought it endearing. I am MiMi to the grandkids, Mama to my sons, and Mamma Debbie to all their friends. I'll call my boys Son 1, 2, and 3. The oldest being Son1. Not that numbers matter; they're all #1 to me.

Anyway, we have this bonfire thing we do, my three sons & I. We build a bonfire and roast wieners, toast marshmallows, or just burn a really big fire, and drink beer. (I don't usually drink beer, but a wine glass is not proper etiquette at bonfires.) Once the flame no longer needs tending, my boys love to tell chilling stories. It's a family tradition.

The scary part is when they divulge what they did, mostly behind my back, when they were young. I had lived with the illusion of being super-mom, envied by Mrs. Cleaver on "Leave it to Beaver." Carol Brady and Aunt Bea had nothing on me. I baked cookies too! But the more bonfire rituals, the more I began to wonder: Where the *meadow muffins was* "I" when all this was going on? Who knows where RC was.

What kind of mama doesn't know her boys pilfered her wine box when they were only 15 years old?! What sort of mother couldn't figure out what it meant when she found a pink sock, a bra, empty beer cans, and poker chips in the basement family room? I just assumed that their Bad Friends broke into the house, played strip poker, and made that mess while my boys were out walking the dog. My teen boys couldn't have been involved. Just like RC, they weren't like that! Denial is a comforting hideout, even when we know it's not true.

In retaliation for the shocking revelations my boys share, I tell bonfire stories to embarrass my sons. It's fair play. They loved being naked. (They get that from me.) Son2 was almost three when we were playing in the sandbox and I ran inside to refill the squirt guns. I wasn't inside for 44 seconds before the phone rang and my elderly neighbor who kept an eye on us (24/7) said to me: "Did you know that your baby is running down the road naked with a snake in his mouth?" Of course, I calmly informed her that I *did* know that. Otherwise, what kind of mother would I be?

I left the phone dangling by the cord and found that he had escaped the backyard fence, discarded his diaper, and ran for the road (it was a quiet neighborhood). He was the world's fastest toddler. He never toddled; he was an aspiring Olympic sprinter by the age of two.

There was, naturally, a dried snakeskin on the road. For some unimaginable reason, he picked it up, put it in his mouth, and ran down the street. I ran like the wind to catch him, and when I did, I picked him up and he peed on me. Our neighbors must miss us—unless a circus family moved in after we left.

Years later, we were traveling through Paris and stopped at the Embassy to have lunch with some of our former colleagues and Marine Security Guards. Son3 was newly potty trained and insisted on visiting every bathroom we passed. RC and I were enjoying conversations with our friends when Son3 announced his need to check out the boys' room for the third time in 16 minutes.

Not wanting to deflate his pride in peeing like a big boy, I asked his older brothers to take him. Nine minutes later, a wave of laughter roared through the room as Son3 pranced naked through the American Embassy of Paris cafeteria. His brothers were chasing after him, dropping his clothes along the way, reciting their standard disclaimer … "we couldn't get him to keep his clothes on!" (One of my favorite bonfire stories.)

I have a sneaking suspicion that normal families are telling bonfire stories about "that Marine family from the mountains … and I hear they're divorced now…."

As I may have mentioned, our divorce granted me the cabin on the lake. RC got the big house in NOVA (Northern VA, where the jobs are). To cover the mortgage, maintenance, insurance, and utilities I marketed Lost Horizon Cabin as a vacation rental and reluctantly moved into that little camper when the cabin was occupied.

One weekend when my cabin was rented, I didn't want to hide in the camper, so I spent a few days with Son1. We celebrated his first bonfire at his new home (we all have bonfire pits). My oldest son's friend, who joined the Marine Corps with him after high school, (he also calls me Mamma) came to see my son's new home. It was a small farm with several outbuildings. We were talking about the barns and the little stone building just behind the house. My son told us that the stone structure was an old outdoor kitchen converted to a canning pantry, and proudly declared "That's mama's house now."

His friend, Ben, realizing that my son wasn't kidding, became pale. With a sick look on his face, he said, "mama's house? It's not very big; is there electricity?"

My son said "well, yes, and there is a light; we turn it on for her when she acts like she's scared or lonely. She likes having her private little place to stay." Sensing disapproval from his friend, Son1 added, "We even put a mattress on the floor for her."

Ben said, "why can't she just stay inside?"

My son truthfully replied "she's fine out there, and we don't want her in our house. She comes and goes as she pleases. Besides, she doesn't like being inside."

Ben came over to me and put his arm about my shoulder. He said, "Mama Debbie, I know you rent the cabin out, but please come stay with me" just before my son said … "She's a Jebel dog" (referring to the mountain ((jebel)) dog he brought home from his tour in the Middle East).

Ben didn't know my son's dog's name was "MAMA." He thought they put me out in the building and didn't want me in their house. Maybe they didn't, but I always slept on the couch inside, not in the "outhouse."

After the bonfire died, I began seeing the light and realized that I needed a place of my very own where I could easily find my best wine glasses and potato-smasher. I wanted a place to hang family photos. So, I bought a little fixer-upper that had an invisible sign on the front porch: Mama's House.

It looked like a mama's house the way a gingerbread house looks like, you know, a gingerbread house. The same way a little house looks small, get the picture? It wasn't a dream home. It was like having a man; I knew I'd have to put a lot of effort into fixing and maintaining it. When I came home in the evenings, it was usually dark and cold. It never appreciated my sacrifices to make it look good to friends and family. But I made the commitment and learned to live with it.

It occurred to me (after replacing every appliance, the toilet, floors, and old windows) what a big glorious bonfire my house would have made. That would be the epitome of starting over. But I knew I just needed to light a fire under my *personal* foundation and make the house my home. I needed a place to sleep or at least dream of sleeping. I needed to settle. Not settle for a man, but settle down, plant my roots and let them grow.

After planting, painting, and decorating, I gave up on the idea of burning down the house. Instead, I built a little bonfire to celebrate, all by myself. There's nothing sad about enjoying a bonfire alone. But after falling backward into a big bonfire one night, I learned that it was handy to have someone around to pull you out (after they stop laughing). Somehow, I didn't get burned in the fall. But I was severely blistered in the divorce settlement.

THEY say time heals all wounds, and I have indeed recovered on both counts. Now, I'm starting to glow again, on my own. Take that TTT! Oh, I'm letting it go. Forget the Texas Trash Tramp. No digression here.

No doubt you've discovered by now that you become strengthened by the difficult situations you endure, just as a big bonfire in a strong wind is not blown out, but blazes even brighter. Learn to prepare a dazzling flame, so you can symbolically burn everything bad you've been dragging around.

Build your fire, and prepare for a brilliant life. I'll explain how to let go of anything you don't want to hold in your memories. Make the place you live *your* home, make new memories, and get your Life-Back-DOiT! Sometimes the strength within you is not a fiery flame, but just a tiny spark that whispers softly: "You've got this. Keep going."

Ignite the Light …
Life-Back-DOiT

Before your fire (this has been done before, but it's worth repeating), write down all the heartaches, embarrassment, and every regret you hang on to. Put your words into an envelope. Label it "Crap to Let Go" or "Dirty Little Things I Can't Say After a Colonoscopy." There's absolutely no reason behind the colonoscopy label; It just amused me, so that's what I called mine. I knew that nobody would think it interesting enough to open. Not that anyone ever saw the envelope anyway. I am alone, and I'm starting to like it too. (RC and the Texas Trash Tramp rarely cross my mind anymore.)

Save your burn list for the fire.

Bonfires spark your mood and energy wherever you are (well maybe not if you're in the subway or your neighbor's shed). You need to inflame one if you never have. Besides, if you happen to be stranded in the wilderness, or if you're simply trying to impress your new love, your friends, or your family in the backyard, commanding a festive display of fire is an impressive spectacle.

Here's your strategy for survival, and a radiant skill to astonish people in your life: Start a fire from natural sources. You may someday need fire to survive for one reason or another anyway.

To create a bonfire or survival fire, you need four materials:

1. Tinder (fire starter)
2. Kindling (fire getter)
3. An ignition source (the magnifying glass, mirror, matches, or lighter in your tinder kit)
4. Fuel (big wood to burn)

Who doesn't carry a tinder kit? Well, you probably don't, so just make one ahead of time.

TINDER KIT

Includes small items that catch a spark (to transfer to the kindling):

- Twine or rope fiber pulled into thin threads.
- Dryer lint soaked in Vaseline (put inside a zippered sandwich bag and squish it around; pull it apart to start).
- Gag birthday candles that don't blow out.
- Bandanna or handkerchief (you may also need to use the hanky for first aid or to signal for help).
- Aluminum foil (used as a wind barrier, dry surface, or formed into a cup to boil drinking water).
- Matches (make waterproof matches by dipping them into clear nail polish ahead of time).
- Lighter (If your lighter is out of fuel, pull the metal piece off the front of the lighter. Stick a cattail in front of the wheel that strikes the flint. The spark will ignite your tinder!).

If you're caught without your tinder kit, the bark of a cedar or birch tree can be shredded to create tinder. Cattails or Rubber from your bike tire also burns in the rain. Corn Chips, of all things, or any snack chips with high oil content will burn. Road flares self-ignite and burn hot. You are becoming brilliant!

KINDLING

AKA, pencil-size twigs. Hardwood burns slow; softwood burns faster and hotter. When it comes to kindling, the older and drier, the better. (How often do you hear that?)

Now comes the fun part; make it flashy. Stack your kindling to impress.

Build either a teepee or a log cabin.

Teepee - form a little pyramid tent with tinder inside.

Log Cabin - stack the kindling around the outside of the tinder like Lincoln logs.

Leave some open space to light the tinder, which will light the kindling, which will start your fire.

IGNITION

It's a survival skill to know how to start a fire without a tinder kit or matches. With an unobstructed view of the sun, use the magnifying glass in your pocket. Put your tinder nest (pine needles, dry leaves, whatever will burn) inside your teepee or log cabin (the one you made of twigs), then aim the beam of the sun at the tinder nest (through your magnifier) until it begins to smoke. When it starts smoking, gently blow on the tinder nest until you produce a flame.

Simple.

If you're looking for some appreciation and want to hype up the memory factor, the most awe-inspiring way to start a fire without a match, or the sun, is (also one of the most difficult) by using friction. Make a V-shaped notch in a log and use a stick for a spindle to create friction. Rub the spindle between your hands as fast as you can, moving your hands up and down the spindle rapidly. (This could appear erotic to the right man.) When the wood begins to smoke, use your tinder nest to catch the magical spark you've produced.

Or, you could skip the impressive, seductive survivalist ideas and just pour a gallon of gas on some logs, as my boys do. They love the big boom it creates when they throw a match on the pile. I lecture about the danger every time, then laugh with them when the explosion knocks us off our feet. I do not recommend this method; however, it is the fastest, easiest, and most fun.

FUEL

Once the kinlin' is burnin' you can begin laying the logs, crisscrossing them, or make another teepee, leaving space for air. Eventually, they will burn and fall, then you can pompously toss logs onto your bonfire with an air of confidence.

Now pull out the marshmallows and sit on a log (or the folding chair you carry). A dead evergreen tree branch (saturated with sap) will burn like a candle. Dazzling, if you forgot sparklers.

Be in the moment, and think about how you feel. When we focus on disappointments and hardships, we get stuck there. Force yourself to look beyond your current situation and imagine the life you want to build. THEY say that positive and negative emotions cannot occupy your mind at the same time. Choose positive thoughts and extinguish the negative. Try it: think two opposite thoughts at the very same time. It makes your eyes wag.

The best thing about the past is that it has passed, and you can let it go. So, take out your let-go list. Look at it again, or read it aloud if you want. Then imagine everything you don't want. See those unwanted situations, thoughts, and memories burning into thin air as you release your envelope into the fire.

Fire is a physical element of change and transformation. Reflect on the changes in your life, and realize just how blazin' hot you are now that you've survived the heat—whatever your situation was. Getting your life back makes you glow! Your world will become brighter as soon as you release the burden of blaming, lamenting, or trying to understand why. It's not important why. It's important that you let it go.

Okay, truth be known, I have a hard time letting go of anything, so I kept a journal to remind me how relieved I am that he isn't smothering my energy anymore. Much of it became this book.

So, if you have the same inclination, keep your burn list a little longer. It can be helpful when you start missing him or feel like you've lost something good. Your bad memories of him will remind you why you are relieved that he's gone. If you can't let it go right away, someday you will. That's the day you'll truly move on with magnificent radiance!

If you're letting go now, find peace and serenity in liberating your woes with the sizzle of your own blaze. Open your heart to the promising possibility of someone else someday igniting a flame in you. You already know how to create the spark!

DOiT Journal.

Write down a past humility you will transform into your bright and shining future.

Why are you happier now that you won't think about him, or how he hurt you, anymore?

What would you do today if you could do anything?

(Something to help someone? Would you do chores, do cartwheels, do a plumber?)

What have you changed - to make your life better?

What do you want to do to make your life happier?

DOiT Darlin'

Potato-Smasher-Words:

Bonfire, Brilliant, Reflect, Peace, Serenity, Glow, Grow, Awe-inspiring, Seductive, Energy, Possibility, Promising.

10

Who Let the Dogs Out?

"In reality, humility means nothing other than complete honesty about yourself"
~William Countryman

Are you someone who likes animals more than humans? That's understandable. Pets are lovable, loyal, and usually more tolerable than your very own adolescents or other human companions. Pets appreciate whatever you feed them. They never sneak the keys from your purse and then call you at 2 am to bail them out for driving without a license. Animals don't cheat on you, so you never have to decide whether to forgive them.

Sure, dogs have instincts, but they can be trained not to hump everything they see. Do you think it's possible to condition humans to be more faithful? Maaaybe. Positive reinforcement works on humans too. But men are supposed to already have rational thinking skills and an attribute called moral consciousness.

That's why it's easier to forgive a pet. No one holds a grudge against their dog or cat for months on end. Wouldn't it be a good trick to excuse our humans as completely and effortlessly as we do other animals? That could be a relationship changer.

I love pets too, but I've taken care of three boys, seven dogs, two cats, a turtle, countless goldfish, three squirrels (for real), and a rat. I'm just not that girl who leaves the awards ceremony early to get home to the pet pig anymore. (RC's gone anyway.) I have missed my fair share of awards and historic barroom brawls to rush home to let the dogs out. I always had to leave for the leash just before the mean girl got thrown into the pool or the office hottie started stripping after the 5th round of fireball shots.

I'll not miss another weekend with the girls for lack of a dog sitter, nor will I clean up puppy poop and hair in my home again. I've served my time letting the dogs out … like the song:

"Who let the dogs out?" Not me.

Robin Williams did a skit about what aliens would think if they were watching us with our dog. He said they'd know that dogs ruled the earth. Dogs lead two-legged creatures around with a leash from tree to tree to watch them pee. They poop wherever they want, while humans stand by, patiently waiting to gather the dog's crap and carry it around like it's a golden crown.

Aliens must be amused when dogs bring us a ball or a stick. We've been trained to put on an entertaining show by bouncing the ball over and over and over again. Martians would think it a shame, after seeing how advanced our defecation rituals were, that we couldn't be taught anything more adorable than throwing a stick.

One of our first dogs, Schlitz, lived the longest. He lived so long that he became human. He could look at you with unmistakable disgust or smile brightly into your eyes. He had civilized emotions and reactions to everything. His communication skills were much better than RC's.

Schlitz wasn't allowed on the furniture, yet I learned at a bonfire confessional that he slept with son3 every night but jumped off the bed and lay on the floor every morning just before I opened son3's door to declare "Up Time! Rise and Shine! Up and at 'em–Atom Ant!" I still do that to him when I visit and he loves it just as much as he never did.

Anyway, Schlitz became my favorite dog after I moved out so the Texas Trash Tramp could move in. Son3 was home from college for the summer, so the dog stayed when I left. The very day the trash tramp moved into my house, my beloved Schlitz expressed his feelings about *her* presence and my disappearance. For the first time in 15 years, my well-mannered, esteemed best friend tore the trash from our kitchen can and scattered it all over the house! His communication skills portrayed my name for her – the Texas Trash Tramp! I loved that dog.

Ok, I admit, I do miss how happy you feel around dogs and how they think you are the most wonderful beast on earth. I miss having a cute little bouncy puppy. But I don't habitually miss having a man in my life. My dogs never snarled at what I was wearing. If someone dropped food on the floor, they would scramble to clean it up. If I had a *ruff* day, I knew my dog would come running to greet me at the door and look into my face as if I were the Queen of Sheba in a glittering ball of sausage. Best of all, I never had to have ungratifying sex before my dog would snuggle.

> My dogs never kept score
> Or became a hateful bore.
> They accompanied me to the store
> And didn't care what I wore.
> I wasn't someone they'd ignore
> While watching bikinis on the shore.
> They'd give me kisses galore,
> And loved me, not a whore.
> I simply must implore...
> Could I truly ask for more?
> But I don't want the responsibility anymore.
> And ... I digress.

Our family dogs' names were Ytivarg, Struddle, Bud, Schlitz, Boozer, Bourbon, and Jack. I didn't name any of them. If I had, they'd have been named Merlot or Cabby-Net. I called the rat Richard Cranium; in reality, RC *was* the rat.

I named the cat (who adopted me) Cow and called her Moo-Cow for short. She had all the markings and mannerisms of a lazy carefree cow. No worries, no agenda, no commitment. No wonder the Hindu religion reveres the holy cow. Cows, cats, and dogs live a life to worship.

Did you know that George Washington had dentures made of cow teeth? Might I add ... 2,000 quarter-pound hamburgers can be made from one cow. Now you know almost everything you should know about cows, Except...

When he was three, Son1 and I stood watching a beautiful snowfall from our picture window in the drafty farmhouse we rented. I was debating whether I should take him to daycare and try to make it to work and community college classes. It was barely daylight.

As we stood at the window, we witnessed the landlord's cows skipping up our driveway onto the highway. I was eight months pregnant with Son2, but somehow felt compelled to save the cows! So, I ran outside in the snow to herd them back toward the farm.

I got behind them, slapping one cow on the butt while yelling at another, throwing snowballs at them, and flailing my arms (mostly to stay balanced on the slippery slope). Stepping into a fresh warm pile of natural fertilizer, I looked at Son1 through the window. He was standing there drinking his milk, in all his 3-year-old wisdom, laughing hysterically at me. It made me wonder ... if cows laughed, would milk come out of their nose too?

But I swear, I haven't chased cows since then. Son1 remembered that day and told the story to his brothers over the years. Hence, the legend of my cow herding became family folklore.

Nearly 30 years later, Son1 and I were standing out in the field of his new farm, planning our next bonfire with Son3 on the phone. Suddenly, Son1 started running toward the neighbor's farm. I took off behind him and was close enough to hear him tell Son3, "I gotta go! Mama's chasing cows through the field again!"

Of course, Son3 remembered that I had a history of chasing cows. He couldn't resist calling brother2 before learning the entire story. Naturally, both sons put something on Facebook about Mama chasing cows. It was the dang *dog* who was chasing cows, not me (this time). If you recall, "Mama" is what my boys call me, but "Mama" was also my son's dog.

Another time, Son1 told Son2 "I spent $360 today for Mama's stitches; she was crawling under the barbed wire fence and ripped her side open." My boys love to share "Mama's" adventures with the world, so the cyberworld rumors started again. Mama (the dog) and social media have ruined my reputation and stripped me of all dignity.

I told Son1, after that last incident, that if his dog should ever die, he was not to tell his brothers or post on Facebook that "mama died today." He was to let *me* report that his dog was hit by a car or trampled by a herd of cattle so no one would assume it was *their* mama.

I made him vow that if he should ever refer to Mama the dog as a bitch, he was to be perfectly clear that the bitch had four legs. How is it that something as innocent and loyal as a dog could be called a bitch anyway? I knew I wasn't a bitch, and no one ever called me that (to my face). But it got me to thinking. Maybe I wasn't completely adorable the last few years of our marriage.

I wasn't a dog, but I wasn't a pussycat either. I may not have buried the bone after a few of RC's infidelities. I said I forgave him, but during the last few years of marriage, I dug up some trash and scattered it into the conversation. I may have even started growling when RC criticized everything about me.

I ran to mom with the boys for three months after he made out with my girlfriend at our Halloween party. My bite became worse than my bark after a while, and I put him in the doghouse the last year of our marriage after I found out about the Texas Trash Tramp. She was a dog; appropriate, right?

Maybe (at the end) I wasn't the puppy love RC married. But I wasn't the bitch who humped him the last two years he was married to me either. I guess

I had a hard time letting go of the things he (and that falsie floozie) took from me. That's the only bone I'll toss him.

Most of my friends and family have a dog or a cat, at least one. I have fish in my pond. Every friend and family gathering includes dogs running in and out with conversations about when whose dog did what where. I would try to join the conversation but got no feedback when I mentioned how one silly little goldfish in my pond was chasing my largest koi, and another one just swam over beside them while all the other fish ... and ... I'd lose everyone's interest just before I got to the good part (without creating a splash).

To feel like part of the party, I needed to discuss dog doings. The sad truth was—no one cared anything about my fish. I had no choice but to adopt an imaginary dog. Rufus.

Now when 15 minutes of conversation is about the dogs, I tell Rufus stories. I have a riding crop (it's perfectly flimsy with a loop on one end). It serves as a leash for my (imaginary) dog, and the only evidence of his presence, really.

I let Rufus (pronounced Roooof-us) lead me around to bushes and I struggle with him when he starts smelling the butts of my friends and family. It's terribly embarrassing when he sticks his nose in the crotch of a complete stranger. We're working on that in obedience school. My boys enrolled me.

When my granddaughter had brain surgery for a cancerous tumor, I took Rufus to the hospital to visit her. She was lying in bed and couldn't see the floor. Rufus pulled me into her hospital room in a big rush and I had to keep him from jumping on her. My granddaughter smiled the sweetest smile. But she didn't laugh.

She had previously met Rufus and I don't think she liked him all that much, so I was barking up the wrong tree trying to entertain her with Rufus. I'm pretty sure she thinks I'm the biggest nut on our family tree, and that cracks me up.

When Rufus ran away last year, I made signs to post in my family's neighborhoods. Although he isn't a dachshund, (sometimes known as a wiener dog) I posted the photo of a hotdog on the "Lost Dog" signs so people would recognize him. My friends loved it, but my family stopped paying attention to Rufus altogether after that.

I think they were afraid that my invisible dog disorder could somehow be contagious.

For months after his disappearance, I started taking walks in search of Rufus. I would sometimes speed walk (backward in case he was following me). I finally found him in the bed of my truck. The benefit of chasing after Rufus was losing a little bit of my winter coat, so I decided to reward him by taking him with me on a few walks.

Finding Rufus prodded me to write a Limerick:

> One day I took Rufus for a walk
> Neighbors we passed would snicker and gawk
> I'd smile and give him a pat
> They were frightened by that
> But it gave us a reason to talk

Walking, with or without a dog, is a wonderful escape to lift your spirits and lower your weight, and it's as easy as taking one step and then putting the other foot in front. Repeat the "one foot in front of the other" technique with a positive attitude and you will be on your path to getting your Life Back – DOiT.

Let yourself out
Life-Back-DOiT

I'll bet you're still hearing, "who let the dogs out" in your mind from earlier in the chapter; I am. Let yourself out and transmit some new songs into your head; listen to your favorite music while kissing the ground with your feet! Walking is an old-fashioned activity that has been around for thousands of years, and it's free!

There are so many reasons to take a hike. If someone has walked out on you, just walk away. Maybe you can find a new path if you keep moving. To inspire you to do so, I've researched what scientific researchers have said about walking.

THEY have found that walking:

- Enhances creativity
- Lowers blood pressure
- Reduces joint stiffness and arthritis pain
- Prevents muscle loss as you age
- Gives you a better quality of sleep, and helps you sleep longer

People who walk a lot look younger because it lengthens their telomeres, which are parts of your DNA that shorten as you age. I'll bet you never even knew your telomeres needed stretching!

Walking for 25 minutes per day adds three to seven years to your life. Even smokers can increase their life span by walking regularly. Walking increases metabolism, helps control type 2 diabetes, and improves your response to insulin, which can help reduce belly fat. Don't carry it around, walk it off!

New studies show that several 10-minute brisk walks can be as helpful as one longer walk. That means you can't use time as an excuse. Walk as long as you can, as often as you can.

Choose your walking style and take care of your body (it's the only place you perpetually live).

Take Baby Steps. If you haven't moved your body for a while, just walk around a block. It's that easy. Your body, but not those boots, were made for walking, so make sure you wear good walking shoes. *"One step at a time is good walking"* ~*Chinese proverb.*

Walk Like a Woman. Hold your tummy in and stick your chest out. RWalkoll your shoulders back, hold your head high, and swing your arms back and forth, not side to side like a prissy sissy. Leave your back heel on the ground for a microsecond and roll through the back foot to stretch your arch with every step.

Walk on Water. It has been said that angels whisper to you when you walk by the water's edge (in my case, it's probably just my thighs brushing together). But you will be amazed how many problems you solve and how many lovely ideas pop into your head when you walk near a river, pond, stream, lake, or ocean. The water seems to attract celestial feelings and thoughts. Sometimes we're angels; sometimes we can be a witch, and if someone takes our broom, we simply must grow wings and continue to fly ladies. On the other hand, if someone clips our wings, we still have our broom!

Walk Strangely. Change it up and walk somewhere else—like a hiking trail, historical walk, a different neighborhood, or the mall. The change of scenery can change your pace and your thoughts. If you walk around a winery, you could discover your new favorite wine! Or get a new perspective by walking at a different time of day. Walk sideways, or in reverse (explain that at the winery).

Happy Face. Walk with a big smile on your face; it looks ridiculous but feels wonderful. Keep your neck and shoulders relaxed, and breathe deeply while you spend a little time on your feet. But spend this time before it's 5 o'clock somewhere because the one drawback to walking in the evening is that it kills your wine buzz. (Just kidding–sort of.)

Raising Calves. If you're walking your dog (or baby cow), stop near an alluring tree and take a 30-second break from your walk. Stand on the balls of your feet, raising your heels off the ground, lower your heels, repeat. Work your calves each time your dog proudly marks another tree.

I know, it's *udderly* ridiculous how much I've focused on cows, but I just have to share one more thing to *amooose* you. Some comedian said, "Who was that first person to look at a cow and say 'I think I'll squeeze these dangly things here, and drink whatever comes out'?" Eww.

OK, I can't stop. I just remembered my son's favorite joke. (Probably heard on Captain Kangaroo):

Why do cows wear bells? Because their horns don't work.

Ok, let's moooove on.

Walking releases "happy hormones" in the brain, so get Happy Feet. Think about it though, all cows utterly do is walk around all day, and cows are about as happy as squirrels and dolphins. What do they have to be sad about anyway?

Lighten up, tighten up, and make it fun. It takes a commitment, very little effort, and some motivation, but you can DOiT.

DOiT Journal.

Take a walk, and when you return…

What did you see that came back with you?

Did you think of something you wanted to write down? (Bet you did.)

Potato-Smasher-Words:

Carefree, Adventure, Angels, Happy, Motivation, Grow, Glow, Forgave, Reward, Kissing, Sleep, Prissy, Lovely, Winery.

11

Get Outta the Dumps

"If humility does not precede all that we do, our efforts are fruitless."
~St Augustine

Do you realize that hard feelings create a backup of wasted emotion? Bitterness blocks your ability to recognize the allure of everyday treasures … the simple pleasures of life. It's like your mind is constipated.

If there's too much garbage in your mind, the clutter will block your happy thoughts. You already know that your mind allows you to choose to either be happy or sad, not both. Glad or mad. One or the other.

What should you do? That's an obvious choice. Throw debris to the wind. There's no room for gloominess when you decide to be content and let cheerfulness be your chosen constitution. At least for today, focus on what you want in your life, and forget about how you've been wronged or discarded.

Life will get better when you coast for a while. Then take the wheel and drive your life forward toward enjoyment and peace of mind. You're in control.

Now that I live in a rural area, I have the privilege of taking my trash to the dump every week. Talk about an exhilarating lifestyle! Okay, one of my least rewarding tasks is waste management. That, and deep drain hair removal. But I'm the one who does it, and I do it with jubilation. That's my choice.

Sending trash to the curb was once one of the few "Man Jobs" I could delegate with authority. It must be an evolutionary progression because most women have that power.

Trash handling became a much more pleasant task (as if being an unpaid sanitary engineer could get any more pleasant) when I got my truck. Hauling trash in my car left a bad smell. I appreciate my truck bed more than some people love posting their pets and food on social media.

Wild animals pull dirty little pranks on me by ripping my trash bags open in the back of my truck before I get them to the dump. So, I retaliated by purchasing 55-gallon contractor bags, which don't tear so easily and hold heavier loads. Maybe that wasn't such a good idea after all.

It's strange, but this little chapter of my life has nothing to do with coffee cups or wine glasses. So, fill your wine glass while I finish telling you about my truck and my garbage. You must be on the edge of your seat by now!

Anyway, I always recycle my wine bottles at the dump. After my good deed, I skillfully backed up to the dumpster—well, actually into the dumpster, for another noticeable dent in my bumper. I need a bumper for my bumper.

I climbed into the bed of my truck and heaved the heavy-duty contractor bags into the containers beneath my tailgate, eyeing those perfectly good 2x4s below. My last bag must have had a small decaying ape in it because I swear it weighed 88 pounds and smelled like sunbaked road-kill marinating in sewer gas. There was no way I could lift it. Instead, I skillfully leveraged the power of my density to swing it backward, putting my body weight into heaving it over the tailgate.

Experiencing another one of those slow-motion, out-of-body/out-of-mind experiences, I followed my bag into the dumpster onto a huge pile of insulation and other unidentifiable debris. It may be better described as an "ahhhh shit" moment followed by several other phrases I don't usually use. Pain always makes you want to curse, doesn't it?

But the good news is, I retrieved six nice 2x4s with nails in them, only needed five stitches, and am now current on my tetanus shot for another 10 years. That's another example of finding good in the bad. Here is a helpful tip: Hydrogen Peroxide removes blood from truck upholstery and clothing incredibly well. Not to mention, watching the bubbling action on your wounds can be very entertaining if your life is as uneventful as mine.

You may find it interesting that the longest word you can type with your right hand is the European wildflower "johnny-jump-up." That's useful to know if your left hand is bandaged in stitches.

You know I digress, so you may not be surprised that my tangled mind fell into the thought that RC is probably still trained to take out the trash while his unemployed, scrawny, superficial, snotty slut-wife wouldn't pull out a 55-gallon bag from the box for fear of breaking a nail. Ha, she probably hasn't had a tetanus shot for 16 years, and I guarantee you she doesn't have as many beautiful wine glasses as I do.

Don't you just cringe when those unrelated thoughts creep back into your life? I can't seem to help myself! I hope you're doing better (than I am) at getting over the comparisons. Let's dispose of the rest of the garbage in our heads so we can move on. By shifting your focus from desperate victim to independent goddess, you can start another day with a clean bag of tricks.

I'll always know she's just a hoity-toity trash tramp cruising around in her Mercedes, and I have a truck ... and a great recipe for dump salad. Now I'm done trashing her. Today.

The following recipe is one of my boys' favorites, and it's easy to make. Whenever you throw yourself into a dumpster (it could happen), look at the other side of the situation: It's undoubtedly entertaining for other people. There. You've done something fruitful. No matter how bad things may look, finding treasure in the trash proves that you are on your way to getting your Life-Back-DOiT.

Lettuce Enjoy a
Life-Back-DOiT

Whether you dumped someone or they ditched you is irrelevant. Your goal is to toss the trash for a healthier lifestyle (and mindset). When your mind is healthy, your body will be too. I'm not talking about drinking enhanced water and eating salad. Although, anything "salad" must be healthy, right? That's why I keep a Fruit & Salad Bar stocked with celery, olives, lemons, and limes to garnish my cocktails. That's healthy.

This salad needs a-dressing; there are some calories involved. But when served in a lovely crystal bowl, the calories don't show, and it's an impressive dessert. Just thought I'd toss that out there.

It's healthier to use fresh instead of canned fruits. I added mango to the original recipe after my divorce because I liked saying: Let that mango! Ahem … I digress, again.

DUMP SALAD:

- 1 cup of cherries or strawberries (or a can of pie filling if you feel indulgent)
- 1 lg. can crushed pineapple (drained)
- ½ cup dried mango
- 1 can Eagle Brand condensed milk
- 1 (8 oz.) container whipped topping
- 2 c. miniature marshmallows
- 1 ½ c. chopped pecans
- 1 ½ c. flaked coconut

Dump ingredients together and refrigerate for several hours. It tastes better with coffee than with wine. But it is also washed down very tastefully with milk in a nice wine glass.

BONUS: Leftover Dump Salad has a pleasing smell; heck, I'll go so far as to say that it freshens the trash. I've become keenly aware of garbage odor. One of the many benefits of dried fruit is the lack of smell. I like sharing fruity knowledge, especially the benefits of dried fruit. It's all about raisin' awareness.

DOiT Journal.

Empty the trash in your head to make room for sweeter thoughts.
What three unhappy thoughts will you toss today?
Now, make a Happy List to fill your mind.

Take a look at some of my **Happy Thoughts**
to encourage your enlightenment:

- Snow
- Puppies
- Sushi, Caramel, Curry
- Flowing Water, Flowers, Rocks
- Sunshine
- Thunderstorms
- Autumn
- Laughing Babies
- People who smile back
- Massage
- Snow skiing, Hot-buttered-rum in front of a fire
- A smooth-cantering horse
- Sailing on a windy day
- Candlelight
- Cows
- (Good) Poetry
- Floating in water on a hot sunny day
- Romance, Inspiring conversation
- Laughing until I cry
- Anticipation
- Waterfalls
- Feeling wanted/loved/needed
- Sharing
- Getting lost in a book
- Roller Coasters, Ferris wheels, Cotton-candy
- Anything good that takes my breath...

Sometimes you don't even realize what you love until you write it down.
Write it to someone you want to tell or write it to yourself.

I love...

(List it)

Potato-Smasher-Words:

Treasures, Happy, Glad, Wine, Simple, Optimistic, Sunshine, Exhilarating, Jubilation, Nice, Entertaining, Mango, Refreshing, Fruitful, Wine.

You may notice some repetitive potato-smasher-words. That's because some words are just too good to leave behind (like wine).

12

Snoring Alone

"Humility, like the darkness, reveals the heavenly lights."
~Henry David Thoreau

Even if you have moved on, you still feel alone sometimes, don't you? Everyone does. There are different degrees of alone. You can be separated, isolated, free, abandoned, single, or unaccompanied. Alone can mean taking time for yourself, for solitude, or alone can be lonely. But when you're truly alone, you're just simply alone, and you know it.

That's not always a bad thing. Me-time gives you the chance to do what you want, when you want, the way you choose to do it. You don't have to please anyone or apologize for anything. If you don't want to make the bed, who will know?

Sometimes, you get a lot more accomplished by yourself. If you're stuck doing something you don't want to do (on your own), suck it up and DOiT. Sometimes that's all you can do.

The unsettling storms in our lives can clear a path to a new beginning. Find the silver lining (there is one) and live with hope in your heart. Stop feeling lost, and stop feeling less capable or less valuable than the woman who took your place. Learn to be happy with yourself by learning who you are.

"I regret spending quality time with myself to reflect and think clearly," said no one ever.

On the coldest spring night I could remember, I was alone, wishing I'd built a fire in my fireplace. If only I'd known that a sudden storm would overtake me, I could have gathered dry wood earlier in the day. But I didn't.

The thought of tripping through the woods on a dark stormy night (with a flashlight using last year's batteries) in pursuit of wet twigs; well, it just wasn't something I wanted to do. I stood at the window watching the crazy sideways rain by myself.

At a time like this, a song usually gets caught in my head. That night my brain pulled out the little ditty:

It's Raining. It's pouring. I don't have to hear his snoring. Most of the songs in my head are altered hits.

As lightning flashed for three whole minutes without a blink, I became acutely aware of the fact that I was categorically alone. It occurred to me that someone, anyone, snoring beside me would be better than being stuck in a remote cabin without electricity or the comfort of human companionship.

As a matter of fact, snoring never really bothered me. I found it oddly comforting. I willfully changed the raining … pouring … snoring jingle in my head to "Riders on the Storm" by The Doors.

I snuggled into my bed with no heat, no light, no water, protecting myself from the dark by pulling the blankets up over my shoulders. The wind was raging, the rain was pounding. It was almost stimulating. Hail bounced off my tin roof. For a while, it was louder than the continuous rumble of thunder. It was darker than night.

Prolonged lightning lit the room again, sparking my creativity. I wrote by candlelight on my notepad: "As much as we like to define ourselves, we don't want to be categorized. 'Single' is not a status. 'Solo' is just a word describing someone with no partner during life's most turbulent eruptions."

That was dark. I started with the intention of writing something hopeful. But the song in my head changed to Simon & Garfunkel's "The Sound of Silence" as the world instantly became strangely still and excruciatingly quiet. Deafening silence overwhelmed me.

Without warning, I was aggressively invaded by a monster flying insect on steroids. I hadn't even seen a gnat this season, and suddenly, in the still of the night, a mammoth fly entered my sanctuary seeking the meager light and comfort of my candles. Altogether, I think he was seeking my sanity. He was there to terrorize me, and I knew I would have to kill him.

The sudden stillness only magnified the sound of attack swarming around my head. Was it the first genetically altered fly of spring, or was it a gigantic stink bug? In the movie Shrek, the donkey said, "You might have seen a housefly, maybe even a superfly, but I bet you ain't never seen a DONKEY fly!" Well, this mutant freak flying around my face was as annoyingly large as a donkey in a closet! It could have been a big horsefly; they are vicious. But I didn't have a horse.

I wasn't sure what to do with my thoughts. That was all I had, my own thoughts. I couldn't see. I had been struggling to find something peaceful and meaningful about the uncontrollable silence when the malicious invader repeatedly destroyed my tranquil reflection.

On the verge of an epiphany, my potentially profound thoughts were turned to the annoyance of the dreadful assault, and how to defend myself. He kept zooming in on my face and landing on my head! I wanted him eliminated, but I didn't want to be the one to do it. So, I wrote this poem.

> A fly came down the hall
> He lit upon my wall
> He was not invited
> Still nonetheless excited...
> Where did he get the gall?
>
> He swarmed my face
> With annoying grace
> Zooming in
> And   zooming   out
> What *was* this all about?
>
> He circled my head

I wanted him dead.
He buzzed me
But I couldn't see
Okay fly, you gotta die.

Could this mayhem in the calm of the storm be a symbolic message from Mother Nature ... or God?

The noise, the infuriating and unstoppable pandemonium breaking through the void:

Was it sent to exasperate me?

I was already struggling with the dark unraveling silence.

Was I never destined for serenity?

Was I going to be alone for the rest of my life? Is that how it's going to be?

Was my life going to be filled with frustration for the remainder of my days, or nights?

Was I ever going to earn the rank of juggle master?

What did it all mean?

It probably meant I needed sleep.

Bullfrogs never do (sleep).

The calm dark spell droned on with the night, and the flying assault subsided just as lightning flashed. Then a new wave of thunder came rolling through my bedroom. It felt like the rumble alone could put out my candles; and as they flickered furiously, I wondered: Do candles freely flicker with thunder? Somehow it seemed to make sense.

Everything is energy. Every thought has a frequency. Thoughts send magnetic energy. There was surely enough energy in my head during this storm to light a candle; why would it be crazy to think the energy of this storm couldn't at least flicker a flame? All of nature seemed to be responding around me. Rebounding from the walls of my cabin, flashing and shaking the inner depths of my very soul.

Was it bad for your eyes if you stared at a flame for more than 32 minutes in pitch-black darkness? It was a long night. I had too many questions. I struggled to come up with answers instead. That was a helpless, yet powerful feeling. My decisions and conclusions were my own now. Just mine. I owned every thought passing through my brain. The only place I had to go was wherever my thoughts took me.

Thankfully, that damned fly came back. I was relieved to know that he wasn't floating in my last glass of wine. His 40 minutes of silence had me wondering and starting to think with too much intensity. Thank goodness I wasn't alone!

Even the fly was freaked out by the wild lightning that did not stop. He dove at me again and I wondered, where were this solitary fly's mates? Another metaphor? Just *one* fly? In all of spring? How did he get so big? Was the fly also in sync with the ebb and flow of the electrical storm?

At one point I thought my lights came back on, but it was just the bizarre prolonged lightning … not flashing but illuminating the mountains yet again. It was wild. This was the first and worst lightning storm I had weathered alone (ignoring the beastly fly again). Yet, as I wrote some of this on a pad in the darkness, I thanked *you* for your company.

Yes, you.

I was talking to you on paper as I scribbled blindly because I didn't know how to be alone. I hope to meet you someday to thank you for being there somewhere in the blackness with me. I felt like you, the fly, and I were in it together.

No, I wasn't smoking silly weed. I was exhausted, frightened, and struggling with my first dose of total isolation. It taught me introspection and forced me into a state of awareness. Now I know what that means. Being amputated from the rest of the world both terrorized and inspired me. It was my first experience *enduring* time alone, really alone; and that night, I started writing this book.

In the early light, I slept an hour or two and awoke to learn that a tornado had ripped through the area, flattening more than 400 houses & buildings without preference. The closest devastation was less than a mile from the cabin. We were lucky—you and I, and that annoying fly.

I lay in bed for another hour that morning looking out at the sun shining through the gaps in black clouds. It was a sign for me to stop feeling sorry for myself. Pitiful and lonely was not what I wanted to feel anymore.

I told myself that I am alone, and that makes me independent. I am brave. I don't need another person to give me courage. Comfort, maybe, but I'm in control of my own courage and purpose. It *would* be nice to have someone to kill big bugs for me.

THEY say that life is like a penis. Sometimes it's up. Sometimes it's down, but it won't be hard forever. That's something to think about.

I don't think I consciously reflected on being single again after that long night. I wasn't sad about it anymore. RC was out of my life like a big black fly blown into the wind. No one feels sad when a pest disappears. I realized that being alone causes you to feel more alive and aware, which is better than being with someone who made you feel alone. If you're with someone, and they make you feel like you're alone … you are. But in a helpless kind of way.

Being truly alone gives you the unsolicited opportunity to feel *freely* and be who you are. Well, sometimes it doesn't just give you the opportunity; it forces you to be with yourself. Hello You! You can think and feel whatever you want without explanation. It's so much better than settling with anything just so you have something.

Life will twist you around and become a turbulent whirlwind, but storms pass, and your life goes on. The brightest way to ride it out is to learn to fill it with light. Seclusion can help you find something good … something good for you. You may discover more about yourself than you ever imagined. That's not possible when you're in a crowd.

Well, anything is possible.

That long blinding night reminded me of something I had read about students training to teach the blind. They spend a day blocking their eyesight, so they learn to truly relate to a blind person. It made me wonder ... if you learn to block out the ability to love, is your heart blinded? Does it still have a purpose? Do I still have a heart? What is my purpose? Still so many questions.

One very long night of darkness has given me a renewed sense of respect for Helen Keller, a powerful symbol of triumph against overwhelming odds. I mean, how can I possibly continue to complain while imagining the life of isolation she lived?

Helen Keller contracted an illness that left her blind, deaf, and unable to speak at the age of two. She learned to recognize people by feeling their faces and could put her fingers to a person's lips to understand the words they were speaking. Sometimes I've wanted to put my fist to someone's mouth to stop the words she was speaking.

The Texas Trash Tramp always has an unwelcome opinion, and her voice is one of those hollow sharp annoying sounds. Her face could be mistaken for a ferret. THEY say that approximately 71% of people who get punched in the face deserve it.

And, again, I digress. Where did that come from?

I thought of Helen Keller that night as I lay there in the darkness. I imagined how she mastered the alphabet, both manual and in braille, and learned to read and write. When she was almost 10, she began learning to speak, despite her limitations. How could I keep feeling so forlorn, knowing how much Helen Keller accomplished with unthinkable impairments? She traveled the world campaigning for civil rights, world peace, human dignity, and women's rights. She authored books and essays.

She worked for the betterment of others, saying she was "searching for ways to help those less fortunate." Who could be less fortunate than any woman who couldn't see, hear, or hear herself talk! I honestly don't know how she kept her sanity.

I was wondering, "Why is it that when you don't have access to extraneous media or another voice, and the noisy storm has passed, with nothing left to fill your senses, that your brain becomes so alive?" I think, at some point in your life, your brain just needs a break to start working again. Maybe the key is to be stranded alone in a beautiful place, clothed in darkness and silence to figure everything out.

If you dare to feel vulnerable enough to rely on your instincts, you should try my experiment. If you have kids and/or pets, farm them out (this may prove to be more relaxing than enlightening for you in the long run). Without them, you will have the opportunity to learn to become still, as hard as that may be at first. You might get an inspired thought or idea to help you determine what it is that you earnestly want, and how to move toward it. It could help you determine your purpose.

In the low moments of life, when we feel immense grief or despair, we can get the sense that there's a presence with us—something more subtle than a huge insect. Maybe it's the presence of our father or a guardian angel.

The Alone experience can't be described; it can only be accomplished by being there in the moment with yourself. The secret is to do it completely unaccompanied (unless you can import a gargantuan fly to barrage you). Take your attention away from what you don't want. Let your experience take you somewhere different. You will understand once you DOiT.

An Insightful
Life-Back-DOiT

Break your routine and experience the person you are. Plan one measly evening of your life to be isolated. It's not as easy as it sounds. If you want to truly get back to yourself, then switch off all electrical power for an entire evening before dark.

No mechanically controlled air, electricity, water, electronics, or companionship.

Nothing but your thoughts to fill your brain.

At first, your mind will probably be confused.

Your attention will dart all over the place like a freaked-out fly.

Imagine it may remain this way for days. Without warning, your lifestyle suddenly vanishes, and you are alone to focus on whatever you choose. Ponder. What do you genuinely want your life to be? What do you dare to think or want?

Isn't this fun? Ok, maybe not, but just envision what you would do if you could do absolutely anything. Free yourself from every imagined obstacle. But be careful, because your thoughts attract your future.

You are starting with nothing, and everything can become what you want it to be. You can do whatever you want to do. Realizing that you are in control of your own life is a powerful start to controlling it. Thinking you can - is proof that you will.

I have a strong sense that you are just reading along, waiting to get to something more interesting, thinking ... nope, no reason to do this. Why put yourself through unnecessary torture when you have enough to go through without creating more hardship for yourself?

Because it will awaken you.

I surely wouldn't have done it either; it just happened to me, like all the other difficult things I wouldn't have chosen for myself to experience. But it will make you feel consciously alive.

I'm giving you a lot to think about here! You may think that you experienced solitude during the COVID-19 pandemic, but you had TV, phones, and internet. Even then, you weren't truly cut off.

So, try it. Be alone and let your thoughts and feelings attract positive energy, happiness, thoughtfulness, cheer, pleasure, laughter, prosperity, and love. You have been challenged. DOiT.

> *"Life Is Either a Daring Adventure or Nothing."*
> *~Helen Keller.*

Most everyone you meet is fighting a hard battle of their own. We've all lost someone we dearly love; every living person deals with disappointment and failure. Our lives are invaded by the uncontrollable downward spiral that something like a divorce or substance abuse instills on an entire family or the surrounding community. But we keep on fighting and we keep on living.

Do you feel better about your current situation yet? Well, just imagine what it would be like if you lost your hearing and your eyesight. You have more going for you than lots of people could ever imagine. Can you juggle? (I can't.) But I have a hopeful suspicion that if Helen Keller had thought about it, and wanted to … she would have learned to juggle.

Just in case, take a glimpse below. I've included braille for you to scan over. It wouldn't hurt to learn something about braille in advance. You just never know what you need to know.

I was wondering why THEY didn't make the braille letter "T" shaped like T, and "I" shaped like I. That seemed sensible. But I learned that Braille is based on a rational sequence of signs devised for the fingertips, rather than imitating the written alphabet.

Now you have something else enlightening to ponder.

BRAILLE

First, learn to recognize: "DO NOT TOUCH"

It's the worst thing you could ever read in Braille.

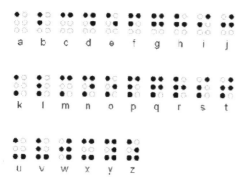

One More DOiT:

Be prepared. You should always have a stash of water and nonperishable goods in case a natural disaster hits. If you wait until the last minute, stores will be sold out of bread, toilet paper, bleach, and batteries, and all you'll be able to stock up on is sympathy cards, fly swatters, and foot spray. Get the fly swatter.

If you feel too lonely to follow through with the Dark Deserted Night plan, then I have a simple solitary 2-hour plan for you. Curl up on the sofa by yourself and dim the lights. Then put on a super scary horror movie. You won't feel like you're alone anymore.

To start your mind wandering or wondering, here are some ideas to spark your vision for a better tomorrow. Start with these, then add to them.

DOiT Journal.

Decide what you wish and what you want from life. Write it emphatically: I will be (enthusiastic, loved, respected, valued, healthier, appreciated) and especially...

I shall become (an optimist, actress, chef, trapeze artist, lifestyle coach), and, better yet...

I can have (courage, a beautiful home, a go-cart, more friends) and...

Potato-Smasher-Words:

Energy, Happiness, Thoughtfulness, Cheer, Pleasure, Laughter, Prosperity, Quality, Wine, Adventure, Love, Guardian-Angel, Opportunity, Daring, Valuable, Aware, Alive, Triumph.

13

Smarter Than the Average Bear

True humility does not know that it is humble. If it did,
it would be proud from the contemplation of so fine a virtue."
~*Martin Luther*

Look at you: living and thriving. That makes you a survivor. You are marvelous *and* enlightened. There will always be good days … and other days. Find and cherish a joy that you find every day. Make it your goal to find happiness and focus on it.

During the moments you think will never pass, just roll with the tide until you prevail. When you get knocked off your feet or fail at something, think of it as your first try. Then try again.

The living will get better when you grin and bear it. Enjoy a beautiful day today. Show your teeth right now, and smile. Big. DOiT.

After six years of divorce (a status I don't stop adding to), I finally started smiling more. I've met so many wonderful people through my cabin rental, and over the years I started feeling happy about seeing couples in love and families spending time together. For a while, after divorce, I helplessly resented them for being so happy. I thought, yeah, you think life is good until somebody deserts you!

Once you get past comparing anything or anyone with yourself, you allow yourself to appreciate your own life and embrace the love around you, whether it's yours or someone else's. Happiness is to be shared! Share it.

Some of my repeat cabin guests send photos and updates during their stay. We've made a connection. They are creative in making their getaway special. Duh; it's their vacation! I truly feel gladsome in sharing the romantic and funny things they do. Well, they don't always share details about the romantic activity, but they have scavenger hunts, hike the trails, and find adventure on the water. That's fun.

My last cabin guests of the year were scheduled to check in on a chilling winter day. After I meticulously cleaned the cabin, I took my shower (remembering to take my clothes with me to the bathroom this time) and headed to the camper to refrigerate my food and pile some wood into the bonfire pit for the guests. Once I swept leaves and cleaned goose poop off the dock and cleaned "Flamingo Cantina" (a festive little bar entertainment shack on the deck), I looked forward to collapsing.

I had spent the past few months cleaning up scattered garbage throughout my property. Yogi the bear made his pass through my land every few days. He liked my little car and left his claw marks all over the hood. Though I can't prove it, I think he must have been the same creature who tore long slits into my koi pond lining.

So, it didn't make me dreadfully sad when I discovered a nasty bloated bear carcass lodged up against my dock down on the lake. However, it wasn't a tourist attraction I wanted for the cabin guests. I attempted to push the bear out into the current with a long piece of driftwood. When my waterlogged prod snapped in half, I unintentionally fell right smack dab on top of the stinking heap of what should have been a smiling rug on my den floor.

I screamed, but none of the geese I'd just chased from the dock came to my rescue. Do you see my dilemma here? No one ever comes to my rescue.

But then again, no one ever did. My life story would never make a good Hallmark movie.

The bear was big and stinky, and I couldn't balance myself to get off him! Turns out, it wasn't much of a challenge; it wasn't even a decision. I don't remember how, but the bear and I somehow rolled over together like a circus act gone wrong.

I was suddenly in the icy water, gasping for breath, considering taking off my clothes again (hey, it's easier to swim naked). Then again, do I have an obsession with being outside naked? I think ridiculous and inappropriate thoughts in a time of crisis.

This was the creepiest thing I've ever done. I shivered more from the smell of Yogi's lifeless hulk than from being in the frigid water. I could hardly bear it! Where is the video neighbor when things like this happen to me? My royalty checks could have bankrupted America's Funniest Home Videos and YouTube by now.

Anyway, I swam toward the bank and stood up, sinking knee-high into the mucky silt. One at a time, I wiggled a leg free, sucking my feet from the mud. I lost both shoes before I made it to dry ground. I crawled a few feet … probably because I was engrossed in my drama, and partly because I was exhausted. I looked like I'd escaped a torture spa before they removed the mud mask.

I didn't want to get into my car covered to my waist in muck. You guessed it; here comes the naked part again. I took off my socks and pants and drove to a hot shower at a girlfriend's house. She said, "well don't you just look like a picture!" Bless her heart; country women are always vaguely supportive when they console you while laughing convulsively.

In explaining to my friend what had happened, I had to admit that I was silently rejoicing to think that Yogi wouldn't be confronting me or tearing doors off the garbage shed anymore. I had been face-to-face with him three times before we floated in the lake together. It was stultifying. I just learned that word. It means to render absurdly or fail to achieve the intended result, especially because of degrading or frustrating causes. It's not a good potato-smasher word but I wanted you to know it.

In my first encounter with a live bear, I walked around the corner of the cabin, and there he was. He couldn't have been more than six feet away. That's barely enough space for distancing, safely or socially. The second my heart fell back into my chest, I told him to back away because I was contagious. After the coronavirus, that evasion approach worked for humans, but it's doubtful that bears care.

He didn't blink as he ripped another trash bag into shreds. I told him he wasn't invited. That had no bearing. My feet were frozen to the ground, so I waved my arms and yelled profanities at him. He just looked at me like I'd rejected his invitation to prom as I fumbled to get my phone out of my back pocket for a rare selfie.

I don't know why I didn't move away as I told him that the raccoons owned rights to the trash in this area. He took a bag of trash anyway (just the *bear* necessities) and effortlessly lumbered up a steep bank into the woods to distribute his stash, my trash, all over the woods.

Maybe he wanted to make it easier for the raccoons. They couldn't tear the doors off the trash shed like he did. I didn't get the photo but managed to move my legs and get back inside the cabin. It took several hours to find the courage to go pick up Yogi's picnic litter.

The second time I caught Yogi trespassing sent me back inside so fast I could have won a backward race-walking contest. Race walking looks silly enough, but my back-up moves looked like I was about to lose a tampon during an attempt to dance barefoot on shattered glass with a bottle of wine balanced on my head. I was afraid to move … and almost too weak to do so. But my body involuntarily retreated to the rear in record time.

The third time we met, I was reading on the back deck. You know that strange feeling of not being alone? Well, I had it. I looked up and he was at the bottom of the deck with only 3 stairs between us. I was sure my life was about to come to a halt in the clutches of a bloodthirsty beast who had come to devour me as a mid-afternoon snack. Do bears like the taste of wine-infused humans?

I slowly stood up and performed a fancy sideways roller derby move, never taking my eyes off him. Knowing I should talk so he knew I was human, I told him that this area was a boot camp, and he was getting the boot! I kept insulting him as I glided sideways, simultaneously reaching behind me for the doorknob and fumbling for the camera icon on my phone. My hands were shaking, and I finally got a blurry shot of him as he casually walked away, looking back at me a few times with another rejected look. I almost felt guilty. Who knew bears could be so sensitive?

If you are in an un-*bearable* situation and find yourself facing a bear or being pawed by a beastly man, here are some proven techniques to hang on to your life so you don't have to Get Your Life-Back-DOiT.

You can bear this
Life-Back-DOiT

Bears have lived on earth for 38 million years, and the largest bear is 30 times the size of the smallest bear (it's a fact). Men have lived on this earth a few hours longer than women, and most have an ego 30 times the size of a woman's. In Genesis, we learn that both bears and men were made from the dust of the earth. According to my interpretation of the bible, women are the only living creatures *not* made of dirt. Need I say more?

And I digress.

If you encounter a bear, you need to know what to do. If he's dead, don't fall on him. If he's alive, experts say to assess the situation.

I can't believe THEY think the first thing to do is "assess the situation." Experts are idiots. Although, if you were encountering a man, you'd surely need to assess the situation. So, I don't know. I'm assuming they mean you should determine if you should take off your red stilettos before you pass out.

When "assessing," ask yourself:

- Are you dealing with a black bear or a grizzly?
- Are there cubs involved?
- Are there climbable trees nearby?
- Are you at the zoo?
- Is it a bear, or just a big burly man?

What else is there to assess? There is a bear in front of you. Get the hell outta there!

You might want to climb up the nearest tree. Even though some bears (all but dead ones) can very easily come up the tree after you, the hope is that they will feel less threatened, and thus less likely to chase you up the tree. Well, I guess *hope* is a good thing.

But Do Not Run.

You can't outrun a bear. Both black and grizzly bears can outrun humans on any terrain, uphill or down. Don't even try! You will fall, and the bear will just stand there laughing over you before they maul you to death. That's pretty much true with men as well.

Try to retreat slowly. Back up gracefully and try to put more space between you and the bear. Talk calmly so it can identify you as human. Complement its coat or just comment on the weather as you casually back up (don't get personal like I did).

Experts assume you're hiking, not sitting at the cabin, and recommend that you keep your backpack on as it can provide protection. Don't make direct eye contact but keep a close look at the bear as you back away. I have found that crossing my eyes helps me refrain from looking into his deep black eyes. I know this from experience with both bears and men. Again, no eye contact; they may feel threatened or worse, encouraged.

If the bear charges you: THEY say that bears will often bluff charge before attacking. (Sounds more and more like a man, doesn't it?) Bears usually allow enemies to back down before making contact.

I'd like to suggest that you not try bluffing back with false bravado and remarks like: "You look a lot like that rug on my floor; could it have been yo mamma?" I also think you should back away before waiting to see if he charges—unless your feet become immobile like mine did the first time. Then simply pray that he's just not all that into you. (Same advice for a man.)

More expert advice: "Use your pepper spray as a last resort. Pepper spray is only good at very close range (5 ft). Wind will reduce this effective range (and may blow the spray back into your face). If the bear (or an unwanted male) approaches within this range, point the spray at his eyes and discharge the contents."

Hopefully, this will disorient him and allow you to escape. Or, at the very least, deter him from attacking. All this, assuming you carry pepper spray in your pocket, with your magnifying glass and spare key.

I never knew this; THEY say to "discard the can after using pepper spray. It may deter attacks, but the smell of pepper can act as an attractor." They mean for bears; I have no idea what attracts men. I do know that polar bears have stinky feet, like men, and that rarely attracts women, right?

If a bear, or a man, is stalking you and makes contact, fight back with anything available. If you had tree-climbing spikes and pepper spray with you and have made it this far, surely you have a shotgun in the backpack you so wisely kept on. Just shoot the bear! (Knee a man between the legs.) Give the bear rug (or the photo of the man in a fetal position) to your X mother-in-law.

THEY also say that "playing dead during a daytime grizzly encounter tends to reduce the level of injury." This never works with men. Playing dead may show the bear that you are not a threat and not interested. Men will never notice if you lie there unemotional and uninterested during an advance.

Experts say: "Once the attack has ended, remain patient." (I love that part; patience is a virtue, right? "Patient" Really?) THEY also advise the most obvious: "After a few minutes, try to determine if the bear is still in the area. If the bear has moved on, you should make your way towards assistance as quickly as possible." How hard can it be to determine a bear in "the area?" It seems obvious.

Then you can lie down in the fetal position for a few more hours, "assessing" your experience while sucking your thumb! Luckily, we only have black bears at the cabin and they usually pour on the guilt with sad eyes, scatter garbage, then casually walk away leaving you feeling as if YOU have done something wrong.

A man does the same thing. Neither a bear nor a man has ever beseeched me at the cabin, but I never lose hope (for the man, not a bear).

Bear with me as I share a dumb joke with you…

Q: Why did God make only one Yogi Bear?

A: Because when she tried to make a second one, she made a Boo-Boo

The opposite was true when God made man.

Get it? God experimented with the first human, and perfected the second—women were the result. Men were just a Boo Boo made of dirt.

I'm not saying ALL men are dirt. I'm just saying I personally have had a lot of mud on my face from being with a man. But I'll come clean; I think I may be starting to like men again, now that I don't have to bear with one.

DOiT Journal.

Every problem you face has a solution. Every question has an answer. What is your big question?

Write answers to your question. They don't have to be the ultimate answers, just start writing. Don't think too hard, just start a flow of ideas. You have 3 minutes.

Potato-Smasher-Words:

Supportive, Laugh, Compliment, Perfected, Like, Marvelous, Humble, Joy, Survivor, Thriving, Prevail, Happiness, Embrace, Festive, Bible, Hope, Bravado, Pray, Patience, Solution.

14

Be Careful What You Wish For

"I have sounded the very base-string of humility."
~Shakespeare

What if you knew today was your last day to live? What would you do? Seriously, if THEY told you that your brain is scheduled to explode tomorrow evening, what would you do today? You'd probably panic, thinking of all the things you needed to do, like fold laundry and pack a bag.

Once you calm down, you may want to tell someone you love them. Then what? Do you have time to prove it? Dang, don't you wish you'd been doing more of that all along?

Every day may be your last. Live like it is. Forgive, forget, love and laugh.

A few years ago, when I discovered that RC had married his latest fling, I began praying more often. I prayed, earnestly, to die. I prayed with desperate sincerity. I stopped binge-watching *The Parent Trap*, that old movie about how the parents got back together because their children orchestrated a reunion. I wanted to believe … Damnit! I *did* believe, back then. I'm so over it now.

The Hallmark Channel is starting to get on my nerves.

Every woman in a Hallmark movie attends a festival or wedding and bumps into a handsome cowboy or trips over a worm and falls helplessly into an architect's muscular arms, spilling his coffee.

I fall religiously, but it's either into the dumpster or on a bear carcass. Where are my cowboys?

In Hallmark fantasy, the predictable plot thickens when you learn that someone's parent or spouse died in the past. Then they think the person who infuriates, yet intrigues them has betrayed him/her in some way. There is always conflict. When they have a snowball fight, you know they have found their "happily ever after." But not until they kiss in front of a clapping crowd, kids and grandparents included. Sometimes they mix it up; one asks the other "what are you doing here?" That big question ultimately leads to an embarrassingly long kiss for the adoring audience of townspeople and relatives who share knowing glances or clap in unison.

I can't take it anymore. I've gained 12 pounds just watching them eat cookies and cupcakes and drink cocoa. Who wants to kiss in front of your kids so they can applaud you? I hope my TV stops working soon. I forget how to change the channel.

I had forgotten all the things I couldn't stand about RC, like his pessimism, his roaming eyes, and infidelities. Instead, I mourned our marriage. I must have had brain damage.

Eventually, I got past that mind game and accepted a job as Marketing Director at Iwakuni Marine Corps Air Station in Japan. I wanted to escape my busted world, one way or another. As fate would have it, my escape was almost further than Japan, and my prayers to die were nearly answered.

The local hospital diagnosed me with a severe sinus infection until I went back a third time, holding my screaming head. The doctors took head x-rays, blood, scans, you name it. Then they did a spinal tap and immediately arranged my transportation to UVA Medical Center for Brain Surgery. An aneurysm leaking into my brain was discovered the night before I was scheduled to fly to Japan.

It was my first glorified ambulance ride with the lights flashing just for me. I wanted to open a window and wave at people. We were allowed to speed freely without fear of a reckless driving citation. (I already had some anyway.)

I knew we were passing my favorite little café beside a cow field in Waynesboro, but no one aboard the ambulance agreed to stop for one glass of their signature wine. They had a great selection and splendid wine glasses. Maybe the ambulance personnel wouldn't stop because happy hour was long past, or they thought I was just kidding. They didn't know me like my girlfriends do. We would have stopped.

How is it that when you have lots of extra blood trickling into your brain and spinal column you suddenly become compelled to entertain? I spent the three-hour commute desperately seeking to pull laughter from the young EMS volunteer looking down on me with that serious face.

I tried amusing him with stories of my air show escapades, and dance recitals as a child. When that didn't enthrall him, I had him confess that he wasn't in a relationship. I regaled him with reasons he should find a girl who would want to date a paramedic. He was an expert in Mouth-to-Mouth, and he was experienced in rapid clothing removal. I demonstrated how the ambulance bed adjusts to creative angles.

It must have been his first near-death experience. Or maybe I just wasn't his idea of a good time on a Saturday night because he didn't seem to enjoy our conversation, at all. I don't remember if we said goodbye when I was wheeled into the emergency room. I think he hid in the ambulance with the rest of the crew. They were glad to get rid of me. Oh well.

I just remember someone reading me the two-pager about all the things that could go wrong. I asked if anything was likely to go right!? Still no reaction to my good humor.

I felt like a bad actor in an overdramatized episode of "Scrubs" as I rode the sterile elevator with three serious-faced characters who, not once, responded to any of my jokes or witty chatter. I truly expected a reaction when I told them to go ahead & prop up my boobs & tuck in my tummy while they had me naked.

Then it hit me. They didn't think I was going to make it. I tried to reassure them, then accepted the assumed prognosis and left my final words for them to share. I said, "Ok then, if, for some odd reason, I don't survive; will you promise to tell my boys..." But for the first time in many years, my mind went blank. I could not think of anything wise or memorable to leave with my family. (Give me liberty or give me death ... Ask not what your country can do for you ... all the good ones had been taken!)

So, I repeated myself. "Just tell my boys ... Uh, You guys get together & think of something profound, and tell them I said it, okay?" The dismal gurney escorts looked at the ceiling or checked my chart with no hint of amusement. I thought it was somewhat humorous, considering the situation.

My next recollection was in the operating room. I heard a commotion, and someone shouted, "She is awake" or something like that. My very first thought, I swear, was "wonder if I can get a laugh out of them now?"

So, I grabbed my exposed boobies and said: "Hey! You were supposed to prop these girls up! Can't I get a little support here?" Nothing. They were a tough audience. It's like brain surgery was serious business to them. I was just trying to prove how well my brain was working.

Anyway, after 10 delirious nights (with an insane headache) in ICU, wiggling my toes hourly and telling nurses who and where I was, I finally told them if their memory was that bad, they should write it on my chart. But they just kept asking.

They finally believed it was me and sent me to the critical care unit for another week, where they likewise tortured me but allowed a glorious two full hours of uninterrupted sleep between poking, prodding, and questioning.

I was seeing double and triple for a while and was awarded a snazzy eye patch. The benefit of my vision impairment was that I had a pretty dang handsome doctor, so seeing two of him was a welcome handicap at 5 AM every morning. (As I've said, something good comes from everything.)

After I was transferred from critical to intermediate care, I was part of a neurology class study one day. Those clean-faced doctors-to-be looked 14 years old. There was a gender gap. The doctor/professor told me to start by giving the class my history, but they redirected me when I started with "Well, I was born a poor black child…" (You know, that movie, THE JERK).

They all just stared back at me with blank faces. I would have laughed and responded "and this lamp is all I need." Maybe the movie is too old, like me, as I was beginning to feel outdated, undated, and not appreciated. And I digress.

The doctor asked me to wear my eye patch for an exam and I used my pirate crossbones patch, earring, pirate headdress, and rotten teeth … demonstrating that nothing is ever as bleak as it looks. No reaction. The class must have been told that I had suffered severe drain bamage, and that was no laughing matter.

One of the class interns stopped by a few days later to thank me. What a great future doctor. He took three minutes to be personable. He asked if I needed anything, and I told him I needed a pedicure and some pretty curtains. I guess he thought I was kidding because he almost laughed, but never offered to paint my toenails.

Why did everyone keep asking me if they could get me something … then not get me something, or anything?

My nurse asked me if I needed anything and I said, "a slice of pizza & a good glass of wine would be nice."

She smirked and replied: "I'm sorry. In this hospital, alcohol is for staff only." Finally! Someone to play with.

It's not easy lying in bed for weeks with nothing to do but count the birds who land on the windowsill and blow latex gloves into face balloons. Every time I hung decorative toilet paper streamers, someone snuck in while I was sleeping, and the room was bland again. My sock puppets weren't a very big hit either.

The nurse who wouldn't share her wine was the first to discover "KISS THIS" written on the bottom of my toes. I wanted to make my un-pedicured toes more interesting for anyone who wanted to see them wiggle every hour. The hospital staff wasn't the least bit creative in the entertainment and activities department.

Whatever happened to a good old-fashioned pillow fight or a game of strip poker? A *bored* game seemed appropriate for my situation. They did, at least, try changing it up occasionally with the entertaining "follow my finger with your eyes" game. No one on my healthcare team had enough imagination for a second career in event planning.

I had to change the rules to a few of their games while I was there. For instance, they were measuring how much I drank. I could understand that—if I were drinking their wine. But they wanted to measure how much water I gave back. I assured them that they were getting back everything they gave me. How insulting to ask me to prove it. No doubt I paid for every sip of water. So, after peeing on my hands, yet again, while maneuvering the piss pot, I misplaced it, and convinced them that I'd not try to sneak any liquids out when I was released.

It would have been more likely that I'd try sneaking liquids IN to the hospital than OUT! Seriously though, you can't get a single glass of wine on any dang floor at UVA Medical Center … not even in the psychiatric ward. I checked.

When you have brain surgery to correct an aneurysm, they don't allow you to have coffee or wine. None for weeks and weeks. No nice coffee cups or wine glasses either. The real mind-boggling question is: how did I survive *that*?

Some of the nurses from ICU came to visit me on different floors a few times. They said ICU was not as entertaining after I left. I just deleted three pages of details of my misadventures, pranks, and embarrassing bodily functions that ICU nurses appreciated. I'll save it for my upcoming Geriatric Conversation-Starter book. You are Welcome.

Since my brain surgery, I awaken every morning (that's a good start) and try to concoct a profound statement to tuck away for any future near-death situations. I feel driven to leave my family with an enlightening proclamation. Still, nothing comes to mind.

All I've come up with is repeating the wisdom I preached to my boys throughout their childhood: No running in the house, no, not even with scissors; if it doesn't belong to you—don't touch it; whites-lights-darks & dirties: wash them separately; put your napkin on your lap; say your prayers; eat your vegetables; call yo mama; I love you, and close the door before you let all the Wi-Fi out! That's all I've got, even after countless years of searching my damaged brain.

Three months after brain surgery, I decided not to take the job in Japan. They held the position for me, but my family made me feel guilty for leaving them. So, I had my crates sent back to Virginia.

A week later, I missed the earthquake, tsunami, and ensuing radiation from the damaged nuclear power plant in Japan. I've become pretty good at dodging bullets, tornadoes, tsunamis, death, bears, scary squirrel babies, love, and a meaningful existence.

My silver lining is that brain surgery is a great excuse for losing keys in the refrigerator, putting makeup on my toothbrush, or those memory lapses some people call senior moments. I'm not a senior; I had brain surgery. Yes, of course, I use that a lot; "you know I had brain surgery…"

Though it has been said before, I have to say again: you just never know how much time you have. Realizing that fact helped me escape my pity party and the daily review of my forfeited marriage. THEY say it's okay to look back, just don't stare. I say, look forward.

It was obvious that I needed to accept the fact that he did marry that Texas Trash Tramp, so I mentally gave him away. Mom always encouraged me to give my toys to the less fortunate. I realized that it shouldn't take brain surgery to get RC out of my head.

Finding my *silly* again was important to me when I could have been dying, even if not many people at the hospital seemed to enjoy it. A sense of humor can help you let go of The X and the stupid slut he marries. So, if you lost your jolly and need a shot of fun, the following playful exercises just may be the therapy you need – to feel like you have your Life-Back-DOiT.

Insane
Life-Back-DOiT

Having a sense of humor can prove that you don't have brain damage, so if you're ever accused of lunacy, just use the following activities to prove your sanity. (Or not.)

Uplifting Things to Do in a Hospital Elevator

(This May Earn You a Few Mindless Nights in a Private ((padded)) Room). I know.

- When you first get onto the elevator go straight to the corner and face the wall, standing silent and motionless

- Greet everyone getting on the elevator with a curtsy and tell them "You may call me Princess"
- When the doors close, announce to the others, "It's okay, don't panic, they open again"
- Make explosion noises when anyone presses a button
- Pretend you are a flight attendant and review emergency procedures and exits with the passengers
- Holler "Chutes away!" whenever the elevator descends
- When there's only one other person in the elevator, tap them on the shoulder, then pretend it wasn't you
- When the doors open, act like you bounce off a force field when you try to leave

Fun Things to do in a Hospital Gift Shop

- Ask to put a pack of gum on layaway
- Walk around the display shelves playing your harmonica
- When you see someone putting something into their basket, ask them "just what ARE your intentions with THAT?"
- Start a game of hide and seek and see how many people you can get to join in

Funny and Shitty Things to do in Public Restrooms:

- Introduce yourself to everyone who enters and ask them if they would like a photo of you
- Walk up behind someone who's washing her hands and wrap her head in toilet paper
- Knock on the doors of occupied stalls and ask if there is anyone in there. If so, ask "are you busy?"
- Announce that you have the best seat in the house!
- Turn off the faucet while someone's washing their hands
- Say to the woman in the next stall: "This is the best part about identifying with my chosen gender"
- Turn off the light when you leave the restroom if people are in there

DOiT Journal.

Write something profound to leave with your loved ones.

Write a letter (and/or make a video) to be given to someone after you die.

What would you say to someone if you only had 18 hours left to live? (Uh … say it now).

Potato-Smasher-Words:

Wine, Liberty, Humor, Happily, Love, Meaningful, Adoring, Forgive, Forget, Laugh, Sincerity, Reunion, Believe, Intrigue, Clap, Glorified, Splendid, Enthrall, Witty, Snazzy, Play, Driven, Enlightening, Silly, Jolly.

15

Slidin' In the Vaseline

"One of the ways to practice Humility is to pass over the mistakes of others."
~Mother Teresa.

Have you chosen *not* to be mad and upset yet? That sounds so simple. Guess why … Because it is. Decide today how you want to react to your surroundings. Drive the detours in your life to positive destinations. Choose to make it a good day. It's your decision no matter what happens. Live happily and let anything unpleasant speed past you today.

Do something that makes you smile. Maybe it's cutting flowers from your garden (or your neighbor's). Or do something that makes you laugh, like rolling golf balls under restroom stall doors and bouncing them off someone's toes. If you hear someone talking on their cell phone, be sure to join in on the conversation. I discovered this idea accidentally while visiting a restroom stall. Once you've distracted yourself from bad feelings, hold on to these funny thoughts for as long as you can. Then get out of the bathroom.

I'm focusing on forgetting now. I've forgotten that sinking feeling when I saw him with someone else, and the names of women he cheated with. I am moving forward, mostly remembering amusing stuff. It's easier to do after nine years of divorce.

If you don't take a determined step forward, you will spend the rest of your life standing on the side of the road. You can watch what passes, look behind you, or go forward. Stop looking back and move ahead to your future. If you must look back, do so only to laugh at your bad hair photos (or to retrieve a forgotten wine glass).

Looking back now, (sometimes I just can't help it), in high school, RC and I would sing to the radio while riding in our noisy little Volkswagen bug without heat or air-conditioning. We got into the groove of the beat but never recognized what the lyrics' underlying message was conveying. At least I didn't. I just obliviously sang the words with loud enthusiasm. I thought "Let's Get It On" and "Get Down Tonight" were about dancing the night away. Oh, I'm so embarrassed now. "My Ding-A-Ling" should have been obvious. But it wasn't.

RC always thought he was soo cool singing at the top of his lungs beside me. He'd bob his head out of beat as only a country boy could. He was too suave, as in, so vain he probably thought *every* song was about him. He always did have one eye in the mirror as he danced with a goofy smile on his face and his chest stuck out.

There goes that digression again.

A friend of mine called the other day to stick a song in my head; she said, "you know that song 'Two Tickets to Paradise,' well, we are forevermore singing I've got two chickens in parrot ties." Now I can't get it out of my head.

Anyway, RC and I were just 16 years young driving down the backroads singing our hearts out when I realized he was singing, very seriously, instead of "Life in the Fast Lane," "Slidin' in the Vaseline!" I wonder now if he thought there was something sexual about slidin' in the Vaseline? But I can't ask him, because his Texas Trash Tramp doesn't allow us to communicate. I think she knows what I call her.

He probably thinks the song "Knockin' on Heaven's Door" is about visiting him at their new mansion, and "Magic Carpet Ride" is about her sitting on his new toupee. Oh yeah, I am *practicing* forgetting. I am moving ahead; I'm no longer upset, bitter, or angry. Most of the time. I'm *practicing*. I'm not perfect. Let me be your example. Don't judge, just do better than I have done. Surely you recognize now how unappealing it is when someone just doesn't move on.

These days, when I sing along to one of the old songs, my eyes pop when I realize what the song means! For some, it took me 28 (plus) years to catch on. When RC first used the air quote signal (you know the quotation marks you make in the air with your index and middle fingers) ... he used the boob-squeezing gesture with all his fingers and thumbs. I know what he was thinking then.

I suppose we all have those funny memories that no one else finds very funny. It's good to laugh to keep from crying, So Move ON. Like the Kelly Clarkson song "Since U Been Gone" says...

I get what I want. What I want is pretty much what I have. I do what I want, live the life I choose to live, and I'm moving on. I swear I am.

Looking back (once again) at my younger self, I know I could never catch up with her today. I often packed school lunches while talking on the phone, standing on one foot, and petting the dog as I nursed the baby. I worked full-time, coached soccer, hosted parties, juggled three boys, rarely missed a little league game or a bedtime story, and passed 18 credits per semester at night school. That was my version of life in the fast lane. Looking back on those days gives me hope, though I can't stand on one foot now without falling.

When we lived in Northern Virginia, my life in the fast lane was the commute into the city. Anyone who has ever traveled I-95 from anywhere to Washington, DC understands my desperate yearning to avoid that ride. I spent eight years on the road into our nation's capital, the only major highway to the center of our universe. Why is there only one super slab into DC from the south?

I mean, seriously, we Americans built the world's second-largest bridge over water on Lake Pontchartrain into a little town called Mandeville. But we haven't figured out a better way to get into and out of the Nation's Capital with more than 900,016 other daily commuters? Sure, I've taken the train, but had to transfer to three subway lines and then walk five blocks uphill to the office. That was no Big New Green Deal.

I contemplated this absurdity with numerous slugs over the years. If you're not familiar with slugging ... well, it's the nation's most unique and efficient means of commuting into the city; an ingenious concept operating by the will of the people, not yet taxed or regulated by any form of government (at the time of this writing). That is likely to change. They will soon tax us for peeing.

I've heard it called ride-sharing too. But I slugged. By picking up commuters, the driver is allowed access to the required 3-person high occupancy vehicle (HOV) lanes, thus cutting normal driving times exponentially ... and sluggers get a free ride to work. It may have changed, but that's how it worked when I was living life in the fast lane.

Five days a week, year after year, my fellow sluggers and I would sit with our suburban neighbors in a space no larger than a closet for 88 minutes (more or less), typically without conversation or eye contact until the vehicle stopped again. It was pure undisputed mutual silent misery. That was the unspoken life of a professional slug.

It's not that we had nothing to say, but there are rules:

- No smoking or eating
- No adjusting windows
- Don't change the music
- No talking on cell phones (no one else cares about Aunt Bertha's colonoscopy results)
- No singing

- No starting conversations unless the driver initiates it. (An exception might be if someone is riding beside you pointing a gun at your vehicle; it would be polite to start a dialogue about what you are observing)
- No death, divorce, or politics
- Keep your clothes on
- No farting

One day on the way out of the city, again, I decided to become a notorious slug driver. So, I cranked up the radio and stopped singing along to "Life in the Fast Lane" long enough to start a conversation before we hit the HOV lanes. I told my sluggers, "Don't ask to stop for Happy Hour. I stopped at The Iron Horse Bar before I picked you up. Look between the seats back there. You are welcome to a "slug," just don't drink directly from the flask; bring your wine glass next time if you expect me to share."

Slugs are religiously committed to the rules, I guess. They remained silent.

Like every human endeavor, occasional departures from the norm are inevitable. One summer I reached the end of the road with commuting. I felt desperate to avoid the bus, train, metro, slugging, or driving solo toward the capital city.

I walked into the office one Monday in shorts and tennis shoes, dripping wet from head to toe, makeup running down my face, without a word. It looked like I'd been "slidin' in the Vaseline." Proceeding down the middle of my co-worker's cubicles, I walked nonchalantly toward the bathroom to change into dry work attire.

Two of my friends jumped up and ran to my aid, but I assured my playmates I was fine. Others laughed and asked what I had done this time. Some only stared at me, not knowing if there was a true crisis behind my situation.

Until lunchtime, I refused to give a straight answer to the countless questions and speculation thrown in my direction. It was just too much fun to collect the assumptions my comrades devised. I would simply reply, "I just don't want to talk about it right now," or "if I told you, you probably wouldn't believe me." It was true. When I finally told them why and how I arrived at the office dripping wet with a smug face, they didn't believe me.

It all started after a miserable month of hauling sluggers who showed an unappealing disregard for basic slug etiquette, and had no appreciation for the sacrifices I made to get them to work … day after day. I spent the weekend preparing for Monday's commute. I filled the oil and gas tanks and tied my jet ski to the back of my sailboat at the Quantico Marina that Sunday afternoon.

Early Monday morning, I applied my makeup, did my hair, and folded my work clothes into an airtight bag. I wore a pair of shorts over my bathing suit and drove five miles to the marina; no traffic. With my shoes and work suit stashed under the seat, I was ready to commute.

I was operations manager at the Federal Deployment Center at Fort Belvoir at that time, and during lunch, I'd walk past an old, dilapidated dock down on the water. I'd never seen the Army base from the water, but knew it was on the west bank of the Potomac. It was about a mile from the office to the dock. I had trained for this.

Puttering out of Quantico marina, I accelerated cautiously into the bay, careful to minimize the spray from my jet ski. I didn't want to ruin my makeup and hair. As I picked up speed, the first wave washed over the front of my craft and drenched me. It was a hot humid NOVA morning, and a slap of water in my face was all I needed to change my bearing. I threw caution to the wind, let out a loud jeer, and revved up the jet ski to full speed.

I was on the water, not the asphalt, and my mood steadily lifted with each swell I tackled, catching air in my face and under my jet ski. From that moment on, I rode the waves with a vengeance … whooping & hollering the whole way … laughing out loud as I passed the Occoquan bridge gridlocked with commuters. I sounded the horn as I splashed by them, waving and shouting "suckers!" I couldn't contain myself.

I had sometimes been just as wet while standing in a sweltering slug line in August, without the luxury of a bathing suit. It was my best ride to work since I caught a ride to the embassy with our ambassador after a meeting in Oman. (He had a limo and a cooler full of beer.)

After work, my skeptical co-workers took me back to the dock where they had visual proof of my folly. It would have been hard to convince bystanders of my revolutionary voyage because my office nerds kept repeating, "no you didn't…I can't believe you."

To which I replied, "yes, I did…See ya sluggers!" And I sped away. They just stood there on the shoreline like petrified wood.

I would have commuted the same way every day if it hadn't cost me $52 in oil and gas for that round-trip adventure. It was almost worth it, but what would be the purpose of going to work if I spent my paycheck to get there? It did give me my 5 minutes of fame at the corporate office, where I already had the esteemed privilege of a conference room on the 7th floor being named for me.

That's an entirely different story. When I wrote top-secret government proposals, we often had working lunches. Pizza was on the menu one day, and I laid my piece of the pie on my chair to grab a drink and napkins. Ducking under the projector screen with my soda, attempting to be as unobtrusive as possible, I stayed crouched down and plopped back into my seat. As I was doing so, my co-workers began to sing in slow motion … Noooooooo…. I loved that white Liz Claiborne suit and had only worn it one time. Pizza stains never come out.

We had 11 conference rooms, but only one had a non-numerical location. That room was thereinafter entitled "The Conference Room Where Debbie Sat on her Pizza." They even called it that on office memos, and no further explanation was needed. My fellow office rats never gave me a break after that.

The morning after plopping on my pizza, my office door was covered in pizza photos. There was a box of pizza on my swivel chair and just about everyone asked if I wanted to go for pizza for lunch every day until I did something more monumental. I rode my jet ski to work. And the harassment shifted gear.

I always ended up being the work clown. Looking back, I think they continued to employ me for comic relief more than my abilities. I'm still trying to figure out how to include that skill in my resume.

I'm pretty sure RC married me because I could make him laugh too. We did laugh together a lot. But he was pretty much a social slug. That's why I had trouble believing that he was cheating on me with Nancy, Deby, Justine, Judy, Claire, Sherrie, Darla, Tammy, that redhead, and my high school (X) girlfriend. WHAT? I thought I'd forgotten their names, again. Ah, well, I've surely forgotten a few.

The signals were clear that he was sliding like a slug in the fast lane on the back roads for most of our marriage. I was the riverboat Queen of De-Nile. If you suspect infidelity, your instincts are usually reliable. It may be a little late in the game for these revelations, but knowledge is never outdated. To give you a road map for confirming or negating your suspicions, I've outlined typical male behavior while living in the fast lane. Here's how to tell if they DOiT.

Move on and Get Your
Life-Back-DOiT

If your man has chosen a different road, not the straight and narrow, here's how to recognize obvious detours in his lifestyle. If he's cheating, you may notice some of the following changes in his behavior:

* If you observe him driving up to a slug line announcing, "I need your body" just know that he may be cruising for more than a fast ride to work.

* Even though you get a bi-weekly manicure and pedicure, and wear nice clothing and makeup every day, he lets you know that you've "let yourself go" as you excel in a full-time job, raise three boys and some of their friends, cook, clean, shop, write his presentations, throw parties for his office, landscape the yard, and fold his T-shirts into perfect rectangles ... Yeah, let yourself go ... Far away.

* You're riding in the car together, and he tunes in his new playlist of songs you've never listened to before; when did that shift occur? When he sings all the words to songs he once hated or you've never heard, something doesn't sound right.

* Insisting that his beautiful, delightful co-worker is stupid and completely unappealing to him in any way is a big red flag. If he says she thinks she is better than everyone else, that's about as believable as a road trip to New Zealand. Either he has decided to become gay, she has rejected him, or you know she is clearly his focus of attention.

* Gifts often reflect what the giver thinks of you. It's just not a good sign if he gives you windshield wiper blades, a food processor, and slippers for Christmas, and you find receipts (while washing his trousers) for jewelry and flowers.

* If he sends you a text telling you he can't wait to be alone with you this weekend, but told you last night that he had to go away for a business trip Friday. There's nothing left to say. You should surprise him with a picnic lunch on Friday & tell him you're going on his business trip with him (like I did one time). I'll bet the "business trip" gets canceled.

You'll know when it's time to take another route. If you're still commuting, find enjoyment during the long hours of travel. Entertain yourself the next time you're on a subway, bus, or train. Try one of these...

- Stand uncomfortably close to someone, sniffing them occasionally, and tell them you can see their aura

- Start a Sing-Along. (My girlfriends & I did on a bus in NYC and we ended up with free bus passes!)
- Make race car noises when anyone gets off the metro
- Whistle the first six notes of "It's a Small World" incessantly
- When the doors close, use duct tape and work furiously to tape the doors together. Ask for help

What could it hurt? You will give commuters an entertaining ride and maybe stir up some laughter ... or get yourself arrested and receive a free psychiatric evaluation. Either way, it's a great trip.

DOiT Journal.

Recall your funniest family or work story.

Congratulate yourself for one remarkable thing you did (It could be as simple as remembering birthdays):

- At work
- At home
- In the community
- In your mind

What is something you WILL do?

Potato-Smasher-Words:

Paradise, Dream, Breathe, Energy, Laugh, Appreciation, Amazing, Wine, Amusing, Determined, Groove, Enthusiasm, Cool, Goofy, Ingenious, Notorious, Share, Folly, Delightful, Surprise.

16

Do you Want
Fries with That?

*"Humility is the only true wisdom by which we prepare
our minds for all the possible changes of life."*
~George Arliss

Have you forgotten enough about the past to live and laugh, yet? When you finally forget how sad your circumstances were, you will find it easier to laugh again. Sometimes laughter is the only way out. It will get you through a day, or an episode. When laughter is least suitable for a situation, that's usually when you lose the ability not to laugh. That makes it even funnier.

When you lose control, your choices are:

- Erase it from your memory.
- Live with the embarrassment.
- Laugh again.
- Blame it on someone else.

There is no good choice. Face it, inappropriate laughter leaves a permanent scar. But don't worry. Like your worst injuries, all bleeding stops. Eventually.

To laugh is to live with joy (and, occasionally, humility). The secret is: to push positive emotions ahead of your bad recollections and feelings of rejection. Just when it seems impossible, something will happen to help you see the better side of a bad situation.

After 10 years of being divorced (just when I thought I'd stopped defining myself that way), I was reminiscing with the boys about a time RC enjoyed the attention of a very pretty woman.

On his way home from fishing with the boys, he stopped to pick up something tasty. She was standing at the counter of a fast-food restaurant. You could say he got more than he paid for. The restaurant was busy and overcrowded, but he knew immediately that she had noticed him.

She kept staring at him as he stood there waiting for the remainder of his order, seductively popping French fries into his mouth from the tray before him. Our sons reported that her face showed much more of a scowl than the admiring attention I'm sure RC had imagined.

As burgers and drinks were placed on the counter and numbers were called for people to claim their trays, RC had to step aside for the woman beside him to claim her tray – the one he'd been eating fries from! She glared at him (without desire) one more time, snatched her tray, and stormed away. He had eaten most of her fries!

I guess there are some things I do miss about him, but I certainly don't miss his never-ending quest for the attention of another woman. The Texas Trash Tramp can enjoy his insecure crusade for attention from now on. I know, I said I wasn't going to call her names anymore, but truth is, that's what she is! I find a sick sense of amusement just saying it. See … I can laugh.

To tell the truth, I don't despise her anymore. In reality, I truly feel sorry for her; I'm glad I'm not her, married to RC. His conceit overshadows Texas and she stirred up a recipe to feed his ego. As John Bright said, "He is a self-made man and worships his creator."

She probably worships him too. He put my military retirement benefits into her name and moved her from a trailer park to a magnificent mansion in the mountains. But I'd never wish for her to choke on a french-fry. (Or would I?) – it just rhymes…

On the french-fry wagon, six years ago, we stopped for fries on the way to my friend Tom's father's funeral. They were accurately reported to be the best spuds on the planet. The portions were huge. I never waste food, so I saved some in my purse for later.

I was with my then-fiancée, Dan, and another couple. Tom's dad had remarried for the fourth time only five months before his death. He was known as a philanderer with a big personality. The circumstances of his death by heart attack were scandalous, and the details were not revealed. The church was filled, but I didn't know a living soul except for the three people I was sitting with on the front row, along with Tom's family. I didn't know the departed soul, either.

My oldest son had died of a (supposedly) self-inflicted gunshot wound to his head only five months before this trip. I don't think I'll ever accept the prognosis. He was always so alive. It had to be an accident.

I'll never forget the weekend before his death. We grilled out and spent several hours laughing hysterically together by the bonfire. We could talk for days and never run out of comical ideas to entertain ourselves. I watched him interact humorously with his children and I delighted in their playful relationships. He adored his children (my grandchildren). They were everything to him.

My heart, my jaw, my gut, my throat, and my fingers ache at the excruciating memory of touching my son for the last time, (my first baby) lying cold and stiff with a peaceful look on his face. He looked like he was sleeping in a pleasant dream. I see it vividly, still. It's the first image in my mind almost every morning.

I'm forever furious that they made me leave him when they took him for cremation. I wasn't ready to let go of him; I still feel the sharp stabbing void of them taking him away. He was my son. I needed more time with him. The despair is unexplainable, and my longing to hear his laugh again, to see him look into my face with his eyes sparkling when he laughed with me, never subsides.

I only remember parts of my son's funeral. I was in shock and denial. But I never imagined that a funeral for someone I never met would have an impact on me in any way. I never cry in public; I mask my sorrow with corny jokes and wine. I was there to support Tom, and that's all I meant to do.

When the photos of Tom's dad's life began flashing on the screen, something deep within my brain exploded and I began sobbing, not crying, but blatantly wailing hysterically. I lost all control and dignity. I simply could not quiet my bawling no matter what I did.

All I could see were the images of my deceased son, his beautiful wife, and his four young children through my bleary eyes. He had the kindest heart. He was a Marine, a wonderful father, and found humor in everything.

I couldn't help but wish he were beside me at that moment to point out something, anything, that could have possibly been vaguely funny in this calamity. I stood to leave but Dan and Tom grabbed my arms and sat me back down on the bench.

Hanging my bobbing head, searching my purse for more tissues, and hoping to find a bottle of wine, I found the leftover French-fries. After drying my face and the front of my dress, I was still out of control, but decided that eating the fries might subdue my breakdown; much like drinking water is said to cure hiccups.

But wait, it gets worse. I knew it was not a socially acceptable funeral custom, but I slyly pushed a fry into my mouth and the hiccup response from sobbing sucked the French-fry down my windpipe, and I began choking. To save you more gory details, and not torture my mind with the back-slapping memories, I'll just say I threw up a little bit into my purse, and it worked. Luckily, I had the French-fry go-box still open.

I was offered a swig of water, and for the first time that day, I was glad to be in the front pew where nobody in front of me would have received the expelled water from my choking throat.

My son used to inhale water to rid himself of the hiccups; it always worked. He also loved playing pranks on me. I knew he was there beside me right then. His presence settled me down.

The rest of the congregation, however, seemed a little roused. I was still embarrassed by my lack of composure until I looked around and noticed that everyone at the funeral was straining and leaning around to see who this woman was, the one so distraught over Tom's father's death.

Was she his latest mistress? Had he died in her arms? I was getting the hairy eyeball from every direction.

How did she have the audacity to show her face and create such a scene while sitting on the same pew as his wife and children? No one said that, but it echoed from the contemptible leers launched in my direction.

For some reason, that was hilarious to me, and, without warning, I compulsively began laughing. I had the noise under control this time, but my shoulders began bouncing up and down again. There is a fine line between uncontrollable crying and laughter. Surely everyone thought I was still crying as tears rolled down my face again.

Thanks, Son1.

I didn't attend another funeral for several years after that and banned French-fries from my diet. But when I got the Ninja Instapot Foodie thing, I had to experiment. Now I've allowed fries back into my life. In fact, I've perfected the french-fry recipe of the early 16th century. It would be distasteful not to share it.

I would give anything to share this recipe with my son. He and his brothers are better cooks than I. But every time I eat a fry now, I think about the humor and joy he left behind and the way he told the story of his dad eating that pretty lady's fries. He made everything funny—like his brothers still do.

Even fries were comical in his eyes.

Life is fragile and fleeting ... but his life will be with me until I *ketchup* with him. Somehow my humiliation and fries brought him back to me, for a moment. My sons have taught me to find humor and happiness in the most ridiculous situations.

There comes a time to finally let our regrets and disappointments go, again. In all honesty, we have no choice. You will never change what has already happened, no matter how hard you pray. I've tested it, and will rejoice with an unprecedented spectacular public extravaganza jubilee if someone proves me wrong.

It's lunacy to hold on and constantly review the anguish of your past. Only focus on the wonderful events of your life. Reflect on your best memories.

The time has come to put on new shoes and walk away. Pour a glass of wine and develop a new perspective. Our loved ones die, new babies are born into our life, our dreams change, we take new pictures, and life goes on. There is no choice here.

Go with it, live it, and find every reason to rejoice! The worst is behind you because you have already survived it and can march into the future holding on to only the memories you choose to take with you. That changes everything.

If you could, would you bring a life back? Well, you can. Get YOUR Life Back – DOiT.

Fry, don't cry - and get your
Life-Back-DOiT

Digging into the controversy over what to call a fried potato, I learned that THEY claim French Fries are not even French! Potatoes were introduced by Spanish forces in Belgium in 1537, and they called them "truffles." The "French Fry" likely originated in Belgium in the late-1600s when villagers fried fish and threw cut potatoes in the fry. Oh, the controversy.

In 1748, the French Parliament banned potato cultivation because they believed potatoes caused leprosy. It took a famine in 1785 for the potato to become popular in France, and the French fried them.

When the potato was first introduced to Ireland and Scotland, it was met with resistance from Protestants because the potato wasn't mentioned in the Bible; thus, it wasn't clear whether it was acceptable to eat. The Catholics began sprinkling them with holy water before planting, making them edible.

American soldiers stationed in Belgium were introduced to French fries during World War I. The Belgian army spoke French and called them "Les Frites" (which is French) so American soldiers apparently nicknamed the fried potatoes "French fries."

Or was it that Thomas Jefferson had "fried potatoes served in the French manner" at a White House dinner in 1802, and referred to them as "French fried potatoes?" In the 1930s, everybody dropped the "potatoes" and just called them French fries. Either way, they are delicious.

More Useless Potato Facts:

- There are more than 200 varieties of potatoes sold in the USA.
- There are 7 categories of potatoes: russet, red, white, yellow, blue/purple, fingerling, and petite.

- The slang term for potato, "spud," comes from the spade-like tool that is used to harvest potatoes.
- Fast food chains spray fries with a sugar solution to produce a golden color through the caramelization of the sugar when it is fried.

So, there you have it. Here you have my new and improved recipe for Potato Wedges in the pressure cooker:

Ingredients:

- ½ cup water
- 6 red potatoes, cut into 2" wedges
- 3 tbsp extra virgin olive oil
- 1 ½ tbsp fresh oregano, minced
- 5 cloves garlic, minced
- Juice from 1 lemon
- 2 tsp kosher salt
- A dash of celery seed
- 1 tsp fresh ground black pepper

Directions:

1. Pour water into the pot & place potatoes into the "Cook & Crisp" basket in the pot.
2. Seal the pressure lid & set it on LOW for 3 minutes of pressure cooking.
3. Meanwhile, mix 2 tbsp olive oil with oregano, garlic, lemon juice, kosher salt, and pepper.
4. When pressure cooking is done, vent and remove potatoes and toss with 1 tbsp olive oil.
5. Close the crisping lid. Set to Air Crisp at 400 for 19 minutes. If you don't have a crisper with your pressure cooker, bake in the oven for 22 minutes at 372 degrees or until brown & crunchy on the outside.
6. Toss with the olive oil dressing and enjoy!

Every time someone asks you for something, ask if they want fries with that.

DOiT Journal.

What are some things you never want to forget?

Remember a time you laughed until you cried.

What is funny to you (especially if no one else gets it)?

Potato-Smasher-Words:

Hilarious, Humor, Potato, Laughter, Enjoy, Life, Joy, Positive, Pretty, Seductively, Imagined, Desire, Personality, Comical, Delighted, Heart, Kindest, Wonderful, Perspective, Wine, Dreams, Change.

17

The Quicksand Crisis has Evaporated

"There is no respect for others without humility in one's self."
~Henri Frederic Amiel

After we've worked past a crisis, no matter how strong we've become, we occasionally endure residual panic attacks. THEY sometimes call it PTSD. But I've found that forcing a new attitude into unwanted flashbacks helps me to stand tall enough to face tribulations head-on and claim my life for what it is.

People develop various techniques for managing a disaster. When you get your life back, disasters may still find you. But after surviving death, public nudity, dangerous animals, and divorce, you get a grip on coping with tragedy. You learn not to panic (as much). Escape pandemonium with a spa day, a girlfriend weekend, meditation, or wrestling a pig (hey, whatever it takes). Over time, you will come to know what rescues you from unforeseen dilemmas. Hint: It's YOU.

Eleven years after that divorce I may have mentioned, my new attitude became all about injecting funny thoughts into my day (and drinking wine in a beautiful wine glass). So, I enticed myself to recall humor when I looked back occasionally. Hazardous memories become less devastating after enough time has passed. That's what made me recall this last RC story.

RC would often go Absent Without Leave. They call it "going AWOL" in the military, but that's what he did even in civilian life—on "business trips." He was just nowhere to be found for hours or days, and one of his co-workers nicknamed him Casper. Usually, it had something to do with another woman, but I didn't realize that fact until our marriage began feeling like I was treading in quicksand ... with no one in sight to rescue me, again. Being forced to rescue yourself instills self-reliance and strength.

If there is somehow justice in his being AWOL on countless occasions, the following incident almost makes up for some of the times he left me without an answer to his whereabouts.

We were shopping in a large mall. He was looking at sporting goods. The boys and I were in the little boys' clothing section. After making my purchases, I couldn't find him for hours! It was before the convenience of cell phones, so I didn't know where to find him, again.

I searched his obvious attractions. He wasn't looking at guns, fishing gear, or male enhancement vitamins. I checked the jewelry counters (one could only wish). He wasn't in the food court, nor was he sitting in a massage chair, or in the men's room (I sent the boys to look). He was AWOL from the mall.

I finally took the boys and bags to the car and found him sleeping in the driver's seat.

He explained it to me this way:

"I walked up behind you; you were bending over, looking at the size 6 polo shirts. So, I held my arm above my head and slapped you on the butt to tell you where I was going."

(He wasn't always the best communicator.)

"She stood up and whipped around like a tornado, glaring at me with smoke coming from her ears.

It wasn't you.

I just stared at her for a second and ran out of the store, then out of the mall."

He didn't bother to explain anything to that bewildered woman. He just skedaddled away like a kid who threw a ball through the scary man's window. If you knew RC, you would know what a knee-slapper this was, because he rarely faced people, and he sure did face her, from both sides.

At a time like that, she was probably looking for an explanation or conciliation! I know just how she felt. He was always running out on me too. He took off fishing when I had 22 children at the house for our son's birthday party! The dog escaped to meet up with some bitches during the party too. I had him neutered after that (the dog). Though I seriously considered a two-for-one castration special after discovering that no one went fishing that day.

I'm sure the bending woman at the store is telling her side of the story to this day – in a different way. Her rendition probably describes the seductive way she had it in the air, and she couldn't blame him for not being able to resist patting it fondly. Otherwise, what was she to think without any follow-up from him?

In his defense, RC was conditioned by the Cold War preparation training we were subjected to in grade school. Teachers have a huge impact on children's attitudes and suppositions for the rest of their lives. Starting first grade, we had to practice putting our heads between our knees under our desktop to brace for the nuclear Armageddon.

RC continued those "duck and cover" tactics throughout our marriage. I'm surprised he didn't use the Drop and Roll maneuver to get out of the store after his hand-to-butt, face-to-face encounter. Recalling his unintentional connection with a woman, when he was on the wrong end (so to speak) was like witnessing someone struggling in quicksand. It was hideously hysterical.

I remember having a fear of quicksand as a child. Almost every TV show back then plunged a hero into a perilous pit of quicksand. If I recall, both The Skipper and Ginger escaped quicksand, and I think Gilligan went all the way under one time. Batman and Robin, even Batgirl, struggled in quicksand, in the middle of Gotham City no less!

Without a barking dog, Timmy would have been history (much sooner). "What Lassie? Timmy is stuck in a well? No? Quicksand!" The music intensified as the townspeople rushed past a cave and over a hill to the remote sinkhole that looked like oatmeal with wine corks floating on top. Luckily, someone always had a lasso or tree branch handy.

There was no quicksand survival training in school, but I learned from TV that you weren't supposed to panic because you'd sink deeper if you struggled aimlessly. It was a bottomless pit. That's the same reason you can't let your attitude sink. If your mind is stuck in a hole, stop digging, don't panic, and carefully crawl out. Save yourself.

Whatever happened to the quicksand crisis anyway? Global warming undoubtedly dried up all the TV quicksand. There's no wine-cork drama anymore. All we have now are cyber-attacks and aliens. Aliens never go away.

Anyway, RC practiced the "duck and cover" method frequently after he knew I'd learned about his overseas infidelities. I can almost sympathize with him. It was feasible that a disaster would occur after I found out about *her*. (The last "her" I would endure). Notice how I didn't call her the slutty, slimy, opportunistic, skanky, flaky, falsified, fricking fake Texas trash tramp bimbo bitch? I'm moving on. You are witnessing progress here my friend. No room for catastrophizes left in my thoughts.

Let's be free of fear and resentment, with a will to survive. Stand on solid ground and know where you're going. You can enjoy being fearless now because Gotham City and the desert are free of quicksand.

Celebrate your independence and strength now that you have pulled through. Stand on your own two feet, without expecting anyone to rescue you. Picture it: You, with a bold, cheerful attitude and your homemade wine in a great wine glass … getting your Life-Back-DOiT.

Stop Whining and Make Your Own Wine for Getting Your *Life-Back-DOiT*

Winemaking has been around for thousands of years. That's because it's an awesome art, and THEY say it's a science too. Winemaking is a natural process that requires very little human intervention, so basically, you can drink some while you make some, and not screw it up! It's idiot-proof science. That's the best kind, so learn to wine, tastefully.

Winemaking is legal in the US and many other places. THEY say you can make up to 100 gallons yearly, and you can share, but you cannot sell it. Of course, you must be 21 or legal drinking age to make and drink your homebrew. Just want to state the obvious here:

1. Do not drink and drive.
2. Do not drink while pregnant or when using firearms.
3. Do not drink if you suffer from liver disease, heart failure, or just about anything else.
4. Consult your doctor if you are unsure how alcohol will interact with any drugs you are taking. Don't do drugs.

With disclosures and warnings out of the way, you can DOiT! Here is a simple, inexpensive recipe for making your wine. I'm Not recommending that you do. But you can. And that's my disclaimer.

Sterilization kills all life off a surface. Nothing survives. So don't Sterilize but Sanitize your jug (reduce bacteria). Glass is better, but you can use a plastic milk jug. Rinse with hot water then add dishwasher detergent and shake vigorously. Rinse out and add hot water and detergent again. Shake again and soak for 6 minutes. Rinse four more times with hot water, drain, and air dry for a few hours.

Wine Ingredients and Supplies

- 1 (.25 ounce) package of active dry yeast
- 4 cups sugar
- 1 (12 fluid ounce) can of frozen juice concentrate – I like concord grape, but choose your favorite flavor. It must NOT contain additives other than Ascorbic Acid (vitamin C). If it contains any Sorbate, it will not work.
- 3 ½ quarts cold filtered water (more or less)
- That Gallon Jug that has been cleaned and rinsed so well
- A clean funnel for obvious reasons

Directions

1. Dissolve sugar in ½ cup of hot filtered water; cover and cool in the refrigerator.
2. Combine the yeast, cool sugar water, and juice concentrate in your gallon jug.
3. Shake and stir and soak to mix and dissolve the precious contents.
4. Fill the jug the rest of the way with cold filtered water and mix well.
5. Rinse out a large balloon and fit it over the opening of the jug.
6. Secure the clean balloon with a rubber band.
7. Place your jug in a cool dark place.

Within a day you will notice the balloon expanding. Make sure it is still secure with your high-tech rubber band. As the sugar turns to alcohol the gasses released will fill up the balloon. Design your label and save those wine bottles (and corks from the quicksand pits).

When the balloon deflates back to size the wine is ready to drink! (It takes about 6 weeks.)

Your wine will be about 12-18% alcohol.

You've probably already consumed a case of expensive bottled wine while waiting for yours to mature. But is it perfectly aged, complex & fruity – like You?

Drink your wine in a beautiful wine glass. I don't like waste, but you should leave a little bit of wine at the bottom of your jug to avoid getting yeast in your glass. Don't blame me for your hangovers and other unintended consequences … including but not limited to the urge or attempt to pole dance, losing your money at poker, regrettable hookups, or encounters with quicksand (real or imagined).

DOiT Journal.

Describe your attitude:

What thoughts give you a good feeling?

Complete these sentences:

I am satisfied because…

I am magnificent because…

I will survive because…

Potato-Smasher-Words:

Grateful, Joy, Strength, Elation, Euphoria, Survival, Attitude, Exuberance, Glee, Meditation, Massage, Independence, Fearless, Bold, and as always: Wine.

18

10 Steps to Getting Over Dickhead

Get Your Life-Back-DOiT

> *"In peace there's nothing so becomes a man as modest stillness and humility."*
> ~*William Shakespeare*

> *"The same goes for women … Especially the humility part."*
> ~*Debbie Craig*

Now that you can escape a balcony, communicate with a fly, compliment yourself, outsmart a bear, translate English to Hillbilly, and make wine … there's not much left to do but to get your life back!

I'm a professional survivor of divorce humility, so while I don't want to sound commanding or pushy … just do what I tell you, OK? I say that with the most nurturing intentions because I have proof that it will enrich your efforts to get over dick-head.

Being ousted isn't easy. It is freaking traumatic and there is no clear path to discovery or recovery (obviously).

To contradict my confession that there are no real answers, I have outlined a simple strategy for YOU to get your life back. This recovery system is as haphazard as the reality of living life, in your free-willed way, while feeling the pain, finding the strength, and establishing your chosen path toward your special purpose. That sounds so much more complicated than it is.

I hope the previous DOITs have cleared some of life's obstacles for you. You should know how to start a fire without matches and cook up a tasty squirrel. You have new ideas to pre-plan your most spectacular funeral, pamper yourself, and dance naked with dignity and finesse. The following 10 Steps to Getting Over Dick Head are your final combined DOiT and may be the most productive yet.

Imagine while rediscovering your life that you have no friends, family, or pets to care for. Just indulge yourself and find some alone time to do these exercises.

We women can endure the trauma of turning 30, pap smears, aging parents, saggy boobs, menopause, thinning eyebrows, and cellulite. That's just a smither of what gives us unbelievable guts and grit. Divorce should be a walk in the park. It's more like a race in the dark. But like childbirth, just realize that no one can do it for you, countless other women have done it, and you can too! You're never alone. You never have been, even if your only companion was a gargantuan fly keeping you company during a thunderstorm.

Change moves you forward. Progress with purpose, rather than simply letting life knock you around into whomever you will become next. Take a spin, turn the corner, let it go, and Get Your Life-Back-DOiT.

DOiT Journal.

The best thing about being me is....

I know I'm getting my life back because:

What are your favorite things about yourself? (Courage, Ability, Determination?)

Potato-Smasher-Words:

Communicate, Compliment, Nurturing, Happiness, Healing, Laughter, Forgiveness, Strength, Redemption, Pride, Hope, Enrich, Finesse, DOiT.

10 Steps to Getting Over Dickhead...Get Your

Life-Back-DOiT!

1. Cry Baby Cry
2. Breathe
3. You've got a Friend
4. Honesty
5. Go Solo Not Wacko
6. A Change Would Do You Good
7. The Greatest
8. Laugh
9. Give a Little Bit
10. Unwritten

Step 1: Cry Baby Cry

Crying is a safe and effective way to wash away your tears. Allow yourself to cry long, hard, and unashamedly. Permit yourself to let go. Give in. Hurt. Rip your guts out. You may as well allow it—You're going to cry anyway.

So, cry.

The crying process is one of the most important steps to getting your life back. It simply works and involves very little effort. Before you start though, remember that you must devise a timeline to call it quits when you've had enough. Get it done, and get over it.

If it's not happening, try these non-scientific crying prompts to get started if (for some crazy reason) you haven't cried yet, or if you're just out of practice:

- Make sure you're not dehydrated (fill up your favorite wine glass).
- Make a crying face.
- Close your eyes and scrunch your face.
- Turn the corners of your lips down and force the inner corners of your eyebrows upwards.

If this doesn't make you laugh, you may be on your way to a good cry. If you have small children near you, at least you will make them cry. (That's why I told you to find a little time alone.)

Now, open your mouth widely, with the corners of your mouth still pointing downward (like Lucille Ball), and make waaaaa crying noises. If the tears still don't flow, try cutting onions and putting them behind a fan. Or spend a good 36 minutes in the shower with water running down your face to simulate tears. Showers are the best place to cry, especially if you can't find time to be alone somewhere else.

If you're not crying yet, you are hopeless. Insult yourself about your inability to cry. I was hoping it wouldn't come to this, but as a last resort, poke your eyeball or get someone to kick you in the shin.

DOiT Journal.

When was the last time you cried and why?

What happened that made you cry?

What were you thinking?

Was it worth crying about?

Why:

Why Not:

Potato-Smasher-Words:

Unashamedly, Alive, Release, Satisfying

Step 2: Breathe

Before you can breathe freely, you've gotta get mad. Getting mad always comes best after a good cry. It gets your juices flowing. After crying in Step 1, now it's time to scream, swear, holler, clean out, throw & break things, but not anything you have the slightest attachment to. It's not yourself you want to punish. Don't ever break your coffee cups or wine glasses. That would be a different kind of mad.

Being mad is good for depression and enhances your health; sometimes it's good exercise too.

How to throw a good tantrum:

1. As with crying, the first step is to make a face. This time it's not a sad face, it's a mad face, so take a deep breath and pull your lips into a thin grimace over your gums and show your bottom teeth, squint your eyes and tighten the space between your eyebrows.
2. Growl while visualizing the way you were treated. Some great mantras to yell include: "You scum-sucking baboon-breath jerk-face cheater!" Or, my personal favorite: "I hope your dick falls off in front of a crowd!" Now, take a long deep breath and let go of your rage as you slowly breathe out.
3. Punch a pillow. Draw his face on it and take it outside. Roll around in the mud with it. Stomp it. Laugh at it. Then throw the pillow in the garbage can and empty the kitchen and bathroom trash on top of it. That should do it. You're probably out of breath, so take a few deep breaths, and...

You can finally breathe easier. Breathe for two minutes. Well, maybe you should breathe longer. Yeah, just keep breathing. But...

1. Breathe in peace and serenity. Breathe out hostility and madness.
2. Breathe in for 4 counts through your nose (peace, serenity).
3. Hold your breath for 4 counts (mindfulness).
4. Slowly release your breath through your mouth for 6 counts (hostility, madness).
5. Do it until you get bored, or pass out.

Passing out always relaxes you.

You should be feeling a lot better now. Beware of the blaring signs that you're still not okay though. If you run around naked in a store cursing and crying hysterically, you've gone too far with the getting mad/crying exercises. You need to immediately skip to step 8 and LOL.

If you laugh or rant out loud when you're all alone, it's an indication that you're finding your gusto again. You're getting past the mad stage. You're not crazy; you're just becoming sassy again. Breathe.

Breathing helps you live longer.

DOiT Journal.

List all the reasons you feel free.

What will you not allow to upset you anymore?

Potato-Smasher-Words:

Good, Best, Character, Compelling, Fascinating, Captivating, Serenity, Mindfulness, Gusto, Sassy.

Step 3: You've Got a Friend

The best treasure in life is a good friend. Talk to your friends. Listen to what they say. But don't necessarily *do* what they say.

Your friends are sometimes out for revenge (on your behalf). They want to help you, and it's easy for them to tell you to do something ... even something they would never do if they were in your shoes. Just agree, then step back and go with your true nature. If you're not the bitch they want you to be, so be it. You know in your heart what you would do if you were thinking clearly at this point. Hopefully, you are.

Divorce can strip you of not only your family life and your dignity, but it also spins up your social circle too. You will quickly recognize your true friends. Don't waste your energy trying to win anyone over. Your mission now is to stop striving to please everyone—and find your way back to yourself.

If you're still being offered guidance after you've had your fill, only take advice from people you would trade places with. I'd trade places with Matthew McConaughey's wife. Funny story: Matthew's wife never answered my letters, (and tweets, Facebook posts, postcards, and radio announcements) requesting to trade places with her.

I'll share Matt's advice anyway: "just keep livin.'" Reconnect and get involved in something new and fun like photography, skydiving, quilting, or balloon animal-making (there are groups for that). Join a book club, a ski club, or the Red Hat Society; learn to dance or play an instrument. Create something. If you make new friends, you don't need to even mention the X to them. That gives you the freedom to practice leaving him behind.

Don't immediately latch on to a romantic relationship to fill your void. You have wine for that. If you get involved with someone before you recover the strength and willpower you had as a young woman, it will be hard to truly find it again. When you were 6, 16, and 26 you had dreams for the life you would live. You probably gave them up to please and appease someone. Don't ever let anyone take your wiggle or your skip away from you again.

Take this new life of yours and renew your neglected friendships. Visit with your friends or find a new one, and ultimately learn to live with yourself. You can be your own best friend if you'll just listen to your innermost *fancies* now and then. Encourage yourself and support your thoughts and dreams with enthusiasm.

Call friends to tell them you can't talk right now. You'll probably spend the rest of the day on the phone when some of them call you back. Others may just think you're day drinking.

To hang on to your sanity, you must eventually stop making every conversation about your plight. Let your friends speak occasionally, about something other than your broken relationship. It will help you move on, and help them stop avoiding you. Support each other and have fun with friends.

DOiT Journal.

Who are your best friends?

How do you describe each friend?

How do you think your friends would describe you?

(Ask them, and use their answers to feel good and become a better friend.)

Potato-Smasher-Words:

Dignity, Friend, Hopefully, Fun, True, Mission, Strength, Willpower, Wiggle, Fancies, Encourage, Support, Enthusiasm.

Step 4: Honesty

Be honest with yourself, as well as with your friends, therapist, proctologist, and family, about what you're going through. Honesty puts facts and feelings in perspective.

Just maybe, you *possibly* could have had a little bit of something to do with the reason the relationship died, fizzled, or blew up. Do you suppose going through this is so hard (in part) because you didn't forgive completely when you said you would? Those resentments dangled in the background.

Maybe that grudge made you critical and suspicious. Maybe you could have been a little more understanding, light-hearted, firm, fair, or funny. Or maybe you were, and everything still went wrong! Either way, be less critical of yourself. Make it easier on yourself and forget. Forgive. Let it go.

Whatever you did right or wrong, find comfort in knowing that our heavenly Father forgives us the instant we ask for forgiveness. That's what we do with our kids, friends, pets, and family. We may still be pissed off at them, but we ultimately forgive them and can't help but love them. It's just how we were designed. Forgive yourself, the universe, and everyone in it, even if they're a trashy tramp who stole your future, your husband, and your retirement fund (at least she never got that potato-smasher).

It's time to be honest, and admit it's over. This step may seem out of place, and some find it more helpful in the very beginning, but optimism pushed this step way back here for me. I gave RC six chances too many. But I was just blindly following my heart. I just wasn't thinking. What was it about his cheating, criticism, blaming me for his shortcomings, and his lack of compassion that I didn't get? I had trouble believing that the one I gave up my aspirations for was bailing on me in front of the world. That wasn't supposed to happen.

Why do we continue to believe the weatherman? It gives us a sense of control, even though what they tell us is rarely true. The weatherman is always there for us, and we want to believe what he says. Fishermen? They just have good stories, and their lies are optimistic. But when you're honest with yourself, it's easier to recognize the truth. That is difficult.

What is happening? How do you feel about it? Think about it, reasonably. It doesn't matter what anyone says. What do you see and know? Saying it repeatedly does not make it so. Get a grip, and stay awake. Did a tornado just flatten your outhouse? That's reality.

Wow. That was harsh. But so is finding out that you've been bamboozled. It's worse than being caught in a rainstorm with your top down. I don't want you to be conned. It only prolongs the pain of facing the facts. Eventually, you don't have a choice. So, get mad. Feel sad. Reflect. Regroup, and go forth with credible truth and certainty in your heart.

Lala land can lull you in ignorant bliss until you slowly awaken to find yourself locked outside naked. It's a helpless feeling. But you are a strong, decisive, sensational, sensible woman. Believe in truth, affirm reality, and make your own decisions for what is best for you, no matter what you have always done. You have to take action. Don't allow what you *wish* to be true to trap you in a damaging, dishonest reality.

Allow yourself to forgive the idiots, bastards, and tramps. More importantly, forgive yourself for everything you regret. We all know it was really his fault anyway.

DOiT Journal.

What parts of life have surprised you most?

What in this world turned out the way you expected it would?

What fact have you accepted?

What have you done to get your life back?

What makes you someone easy to believe?

Potato-Smasher-Words:

Silent, Listen, Strong, Decisive, Sensational, Sensible, Reality, Understanding, Light-hearted, Forgiving, Firm, Fair, Funny, Optimism, Aspirations.

Step 5: Go Solo Not Wacko

Don't let peace and solitude make you sad. When you learn to be alone, you learn how to be transparent with yourself. Remember who you are and be who you want to be. It's not like you're going to disapprove of your true self, are you? Hint: the answer is hell no.

Don't communicate in any way with anyone for an entire day, or a week if you can. This is crucial to stop feeling betrayed and battered. You've committed to being honest with yourself, so tell the truth – that you are magnificent, and you are taking control of your life without notice. Well, I guess you could consider that proclamation your notice. But do it.

Your point of view changes when you're not in the middle of the action. That's why you're taking time to be alone. The best view of the Eiffel Tower is not from the tower's observation deck. Step back and look at your life, then work your way to the top to look down at what you left below. Wave goodbye and be where you are now.

Stand in front of a mirror and start telling yourself how stunning you are. Wink at yourself in the mirror and affirm yourself with well-deserved endorsements like:

- Hey baby, looks like you dropped something, my jaw.
- If you were a triangle, you'd be "acute" one.
- Guess what I'm wearing? The smile you gave me.
- Are you a parking ticket? Because you've got FINE written all over you.
- You are so sweet you could put Hershey's out of business.
- I must be in heaven because I'm looking at an angel!

Believe it. Believe in yourself from now on. Practice accepting praise with gratitude and poise. You need some alone time to appreciate who you are and feel it from deep within your heart. Get busy now and do a few more things by yourself. Buy a new coffee cup or wine glass, clean out your sock drawer, smear an avocado all over your face, jump up and down on the bed, walk, get a massage and Get your Life-Back-DOiT.

DOiT Journal.

I'm sure you remember that your thoughts cause your feelings. Your feelings determine how you act, feel, and who you are. You know who you are; you are fabulous!

OK Ms. Awesome Pants, tell yourself, who are you?

What is the most fabulous thing about being alone with you?

What words are all about YOU and who you are becoming?

Put them on your Potato-Smasher in a different color.

They're Your Words.

Potato-Smasher-Words:

Hope, Freedom, Clarity, Transparent, Courage, Pride, Love, Moxie, Generosity, Cheer, Trust, Joy, Fabulous, Genuine, Delightful, Worthy, Beautiful, Skillful, Adorable, Brilliant, Charming, Fun, Kind, Self-Reliant, Adventure, Poise, Appreciation.

Step 6: A Change Would Do You Good

Space, freedom, tranquility. That's what you are facing now. This is so good. Everything is possible, and nothing can hold you back.

Do Something Dramatic. Get outta town. Escape. Sometimes a change in mindset is simply a change in scenery. Go to a casino, a local theater, or just drive. Do it with yourself, if you dare, or get your goofiest friend to go someplace with you. Ride in a convertible like Thelma & Louise (just not over the cliff).

Eat delicious food and try things you haven't done—until now. Visit a zoo and name animals after people they remind you of. When leaving the zoo, start running towards the parking lot, yelling "Run for Your Lives!!"

Change makes life longer, makes you more interesting, and makes you look at things differently. Get over it already and make a change. If you haven't committed to a plan yet, just get your ass in gear and do something. Anything! Put a smile on your face and get up this minute. Now, move, dance, walk, run, twirl! Or…

Force Yourself to:

- Get out of bed
- Get into your groove
- Fill your favorite coffee cup to the brim
- Fill your favorite wine glass to the middle of the widest width (the proper fill for a wine glass)
- Read and learn something new every day from now on
- At least once a week, wear an outfit that makes you feel special (do it today)
- Physically declutter your house
- Beat on a drum
- Peel a banana with your feet
- Sculpt something with clay
- Cook something delicious from a book of old recipes (check out squirrel stew in chapter 7)
- Learn to juggle

The most important thing is that you do something that changes your normal routine and broadens your horizons. Begin your day in a different way. Start with the first hour. Mix it up. Stretch, read, then write in your journal with a cup of coffee on the front porch. Thoughtfully and gradually change little things about what you do every day and begin getting your life back.

Inspire yourself. Read a DOiT blog at lifebackdoit.com, or check a local magazine for ideas to rearrange your thoughts and activities. If you work sitting in an office, get up every 58 minutes and walk down the hall to take a peek at someone interesting. Get a drink of water. Water is great for hangovers, hydrates your skin, lubricates your joints, and is one of the cheapest ways to stay healthy. So put some in your wine glass a few times a day.

This should be a DOiT, but here's a bonus idea for changing things up: Next time you go to an aquarium, take a fishing pole. That's all. Just carry your fishing pole around with you at the aquarium. You have to DOiT to understand why.

Do whatever feels right, just be sure to move forward in a way you never have before. You are so worth it, and the change will do you good.

DOiT Journal.

3 Changes in your routine you will make this week:

Something new you once tried that you'll never regret:

Write or create everything, nothing or anything. Babble and inspire yourself with absurdity. Write for five minutes. You're good at it now.

Potato-Smasher-Words:

Change, Escape, Wellness, Refreshing, Action, Interesting, Talents, Joys, Thoughtfully, Horizons, New.

Step 7: The Greatest
Perspective Unfolds Your Purpose

Do you ever wonder if you have a purpose? We are all here for a reason. It may not seem evident right now, but if you open your heart and free your mind, it will come to you. Once you notice that there is something more powerful than your broken heart, you can use that perspective to develop your goals. Your purpose will emerge as you find joy in accomplishing your pursuits.

Please watch the Kenny Rogers music video, "The Greatest," about the little boy who, day after day, tosses the ball into the air, swings, and misses every dang time. That little boy never loses hope, and he never gives up. He has no one to pitch to him; No one helps him. Yet he believes that he will succeed.

His mom calls him in for dinner and the little feller imagines that everything depends on his last bat. The world stands still as he throws the ball up and swings with all his might. He misses, again. But his takeaway? He missed hitting the ball because he's such an incredible pitcher!

That level of optimism and undying belief is what we were born with. As a child, we saw every possibility as a reality we could capture. Over our lifetime, we allowed failure and rejection to weigh down our confidence and ambition, but you can recover it again. When an outcome isn't what you expect, look at it as if you were a child, and discover why it is ultimately better than what you thought you wanted.

You may have grown up, but you can still decide what to grow into. Decide that you are the greatest by thinking greatly. When you are optimistic, you attract unexpected opportunities. You'll find yourself surrounded by more interesting people because your "feel good" energy attracts more. It's a wonderful circle to get caught in. When people who used to drag you down come around, either lift them up or run away. Stay on a high level of hope and optimism, even if you do it by yourself at first.

There's nothing better than childish confidence and enthusiasm. You can easily capture it again once you change your perspective. Listening to perky music will help change your mood, especially once you know the lyrics and sing along! Music is like a push-up bra that lifts you with absolutely no effort.

Take advantage of the fact that you can create your playlist of uplifting tunes and find the lyrics online. Check out my blog for a playlist of songs from this book. You may find that your lyrics are different from the artist's ... like Slidin' in the Vaseline. Make your list of happy music this week.

You will soon be finding that optimistic joy of childhood again if you DOiT.

DOiT Journal.

What do you consider to be the *Greatest* thing you've ever done?

What is your next goal in life?

What is more powerful than your broken heart?

What might be your purpose?

What IS your purpose?

Potato-Smasher-Words:

Greatest, Proud, Powerful, Succeed, Remarkable, Magic, Possible, Optimistic, Energy, Accomplishing, Ambition, Recover, Perspective, Perky.

Step 8: Laugh

When they were young, I'd tell my boys to just laugh it off because they were going to be happy, whether they liked it or not! Before "laughing yoga" was a thing, my son and I would start laughing and laugh at laughing at each other. Laughing doesn't always make sense, that's what's so funny about it.

Did you know that people pay to laugh? It's called Laughing Yoga.

Here's how it's done:

- Clap while chanting "ho ho ha ha ha" and throwing your arms into the air!
- Breathe in while lifting your arms … laughing as you lower them.
- Greeting laughter: Greet, wave, and laugh at each other – or do it in the mirror with yourself.
- Argument laughter: Shake a finger at someone while laughing. (That is so confusing to me)
- Ants in your pants: That's my favorite … Imagine it, and do it.
- Another yoga laughter exercise is both stupid and somewhat insightful: Time to laugh: Look at your watch and laugh. Do that every time you look at a clock or check your phone for the time. The stupidity of it may become funny to you.

Just stop right now, as you read this, and slap a big stupid smile on your face, raising your eyebrows.

You may have to force it, but DOiT. SMILE! Now fake a laugh for 48 seconds, then giggle. Start again, Smile, giggle and make laughing sounds.

THEY say your body doesn't know the difference between a fake laugh and a real laugh, thus the benefits are the same. Laughing strengthens your immune system, your heart, and your attitude. It relieves stress, burns calories, and (probably) eliminates unwanted facial hair. Laughter inspires hope and helps you release anger, enabling you to get your life back.

Just be warned that laughter can be contagious. Do you want proof? Get with (or call) a friend and simply start laughing. Keep on laughing until they start, and it will be hard to stop! Very few other actions lower your blood pressure, heal hangnails and medicate your pain like laughter does. That's why THEY say Laughter is the best medicine (unless you have diarrhea).

When you finally forgive, you learn to smile again.

When you smile about the life you live, you end up living a life worth smiling about.

When you smile, it sometimes leads to laughter.

When you laugh and move on, you take your Life-Back-DOiT.

DOiT Journal.

What makes you smile?

What makes you laugh?

Remember something really funny and write it down:

Find something funny to do with or to someone (something they will think is funny as well).

Some ideas:

Next time you're in a public restroom:

- Look into the mirror and make happy then sad faces at the person beside you.
- Guard the paper towel dispenser in the name of a New Green Deal then offer to blow-dry people's hands with your mouth to save energy.
- Sing "There's a Hole in the Bucket, Dear Liza, Dear Liza" and ask others to sing along.

Potato-Smasher-Words:

Giggle, Laugh, Smile, Enjoying, Insightful, Benefits, Inspires, Greet.

Step 9: Give a Little Bit

Now that you can breathe, you've forgiven, laughed, and moved on, I'm going to share the secret of genuine happiness. It's the most fulfilling and simple DOiT in this book. Nothing you have done for yourself thus far comes close to filling your soul with as much joy. It's commonly known as an act of human kindness.

You may already know this, but true happiness is found in helping others. THEY say that giving activates the same parts of the brain that are stimulated by food and sex. Experiments show that altruism is pleasurable. It's not how much you give, but how sincere you feel about the giving. When it comes from the heart, you will feel it, and so will the receiver. That must be what Mahatma Gandhi meant when he said, "To find yourself, lose yourself in the service of others."

Have you ever done something simple for someone without realizing how much it would mean to them? When you see the unspoken gratitude in their eyes and sense their appreciation, you feel genuine connection and warmth. It's an unintentional gift to yourself. Gifting sometimes seems a little selfish to me. I find more happiness in giving gifts than in receiving anything. (Well, unless it's a sailboat or a subscription to unlimited massages.)

While giving is easy for me, I always found it difficult to accept help from other people until someone said to me: "Don't deny me the joy of doing this for you." That was a *genuine* offer and it somehow made me feel good about accepting the help.

There are so many little things you can do. You can use some, or all of the following simple ideas that lead to mutual happiness:

- Say something nice to the checkout clerk. That's always an easy one.
- Let someone into your lane while you're driving. That's a hard one for me.

- Love your home.
- Forgive.
- Really, Forgive.
- Mow your neighbor's side of the yard.
- Share your wine.
- Pick up trash (no reference to people here).
- Teach someone to laugh – do it with them.
- Put a quarter in a meter that's about to expire.
- Hug your family and friends.
- Chase someone's runaway grocery cart (and give it back to them).
- Buy a handful of flowers and hand them out.
- Make someone else's day with a genuine compliment.
- Make squirrel soup for your boss. Give her the recipe only after she compliments it.

If you know of someone in need, you know what to do. Nothing will ever make you feel any better than helping someone else. I promise you; this is the one absolute truth of life. Pay it forward at every opportunity.

DOiT Journal.

How will you make life better for someone else?

How will you be the reason someone smiles today?

List things you do for others.

What will you do for someone this week?

Potato-Smasher-Words:

Give, Smile, Laugh, Fulfilling, Genuine, Compliment, Altruism, Pleasurable, Appreciation, Warmth, Connection, Enrich, Help, Confidence, Share, Service, Sincere, Home, Kindness, Gratitude.

Step 10. Unwritten

Wherever you are, just look how far you have come. You are not the heartsick mortal who shuffled through her misery. You are lively, spirited, and magnificent (good Potato-Smasher-Words). You have confidence and charisma. You may not be exactly where you wanted to go, but you are closer to your destination than you were before, or maybe your destination has changed. It's up to you now.

It only takes one person to rule your world: You.

It only takes one person to make you happy: You.

It only takes one person to change directions, but it takes two people to have fun on a see-saw — unless you're very creative! You are the author of your own story, beginning now, so get creative. Your page is blank. The pen is in your hand (a wine glass is in your other hand). Write an incredibly empowering and novel future.

Be that little girl sitting on a porch swing with her grandmother, or eating a worm to impress the cute little boy down the street. That hopeful, optimistic, sometimes giddy girl is still in you. Call her to come out to play again, and dance in the rain.

What happened yesterday no longer exists. Today is a whole new day, and you are the heroine in your story. Run with it. Don't let your life sit unattended like a cold cup of coffee (sharp, dark, and bitter). Create the rest of your life the way you like your wine: bold, balanced, rich with character, elegant, and fruity with a hint of sweetness.

Whatever your dreams may be, it's up to you to make them come true. Set your goals; write them down; and do one thing every day to move closer to the future you want. Every day, do more and do better than the day before, and absolutely do everything with purpose.

THEY say that a woman without a man is like a fish without a bicycle. That may be true, or it may be something funny to say if you haven't found someone to love. It's natural to want a partner, so, if you are thinking about adding another plate to the table but haven't reeled in your big catch, don't panic or feel desperate. Your boat will come in when you have charted your course.

Just know what you want, and realize that you don't need a man to solve your problems. You may want a man, but make sure it's someone who won't become your problem. Take it slow and easy, and enjoy today for what it is. Learn about yourself so you can introduce the true you when the time comes. Make sure you know yourself well enough; then, you can engage with a new person with a daring and open heart.

Today is where your book begins. The future is always unwritten, and rewrites are allowed. Be fearless. Have fun, laugh, and start outlining the story of YOU today to become who you want to be. Finish all the sentences in your first draft with "Duhh, WINNING!"

DOiT.

Believe in the infinite possibilities for your future. You are brave, intelligent, and courageous. As every moment passes, you are more loveable than you have ever been before. Now get up and continue growing as an amazing person, and rule your marvelous life!

Always remember, you have the ability, the strength, and the passion to follow your dreams and Get Your Life Back, DOiT.

DOiT Journal.

What is something amazing about your life at this very moment?

Name 5 traits you find appealing in another person.

What makes you like another person?

What are your 3 main goals for the rest of your life?

What is your future?

Begin your story there (in your future) and tell how you succeeded and became everything you imagined you could.

Potato-Smasher-Words:

Smokin,' Lively, Spirited, Magnificent, Wonder, Heroine, Confidence, Charisma, Brave, Intelligent, Giddy, Wine, Elegant, Bold, Balanced, Amazing, Courageous, DOiT.

Did you Discover the one word that will change your life?
DOiT.

Do the DOiTs and change your life. You are worthy; you are fun and adventurous. You are unstoppable, and you are getting your life back. Prove it by waving at everyone you pass this week. DOiT.

Smile at everyone you see today ... DOiT!

Congratulations! You've taken some time for yourself, discovered how to create happiness all around you, and you've become a human genius! That's getting your Life-Back-DOiT.

Review:

Thank you for purchasing *Coffee Cups & Wine Glasses*. I know you could have picked any number of books to read, but you picked this book and for that, I am extremely grateful.

I hope it adds value and humor to your everyday life. If so, please feel free to share a photo of yourself reading this book with your friends and family by posting it on Facebook, Twitter, Instagram, or wherever you share. #coffeecupswineglasses #doit.

If you enjoyed *Coffee Cups & Wine Glasses* and found some benefit in reading it, I'd like to hear from you and hope that you will take some time to post a review wherever you purchased this book. Your feedback and support are important to me.

Thank you in advance! I wish you happiness,
healing, and the courage to do the DOiTs!

Check out my monthly Blogs at: https://www.lifebackdoit.com/blog

Dedication:

When unbelievably horrific things happened to me, I'd call my friends for sympathy. Instead of compassion, they responded with uncontrollable laughter and requests for me to write about my wreckage so they could share my preposterous existence with their friends or therapist. I did.

So, Elizabeth, Denise, Lynn, Maritza, Alyssa, Theresa, Georgia Lee, Michelle, Carolyn, Sue, Sandra K, Sara Faith, Silly Locker Mate, Beverly, Alana, Sydney, Barbara, Jewel, Pat & Mac, and Carol: Here are a few things you thought I should share so you can love your own life even more. Thank you for laughing at me when I couldn't laugh at myself. That's what friends are for, and you are the best of the best!

Bucky, Johnathan, Matthew, Daddy, Mama Jessie, Michael, Monica, Quint, Craig, Hunter, Muna, Stella, Summer, Anna, Cary, Mackenzie, Sharon … and my future family members, I hope I haven't embarrassed you (too much, but enough). I love you all.

A special thanks to Dr. Mary Jensen for saving my life, twice. It's a rare indulgence to look forward to an appointment with a brain surgeon over the years, but I do! She understands my brain, and never officially diagnosed me with brain damage, or did she?

Biography:

Debbie Seagle lives in the Blue Ridge Mountains of Virginia, loving life as a professionally divorced mother of three wonderful sons, and MiMi to magnificent people. She has lived almost everywhere and worked as an airshow director, marketing director for military bases, Federal Deployment Center operations manager, and Top Secret senior technical writer for some of the world's unknown oracles.

Debbie authored a Sunday column in the New Orleans Times-Picayune, was a US Embassy newsletter author/editor/publisher, events director, teenage lifeguard, young military wife grocery-bagger for tips, shampoo girl, United Airshow Grunt (UAG), senior census field manager, and systems trainer to assist the Secret Service, National Sheriff's Association, and others to find bad guys.

As president of the Cherry Point Officers' Wives Club, Debbie hosted Nicholas Sparks at a luncheon where his conversation made writing a book sound easier than it is.

When she isn't hiding at the cabin writing to you, Debbie enjoys being with her family, scuba diving, snow skiing, sailing, gardening, hiking, kayaking, hanging with friends, and good wine in a magnificent wine glass. She once shared a bottle of $1,600 wine with a celebrity. It wasn't any better than her favorite $28 bottle. That was a life lesson.

She has degrees and certificates for various other obscure vocations, but her lifelong endeavor to become an accomplished juggler has not transpired - yet. Someday she will DOiT.